Understanding Karl Rahner

Understanding
KARL RAHNER

An Introduction to his Life and Thought

Herbert Vorgrimler

SCM PRESS LTD

Translated by John Bowden from the German
Karl Rahner verstehen. Eine Einführung in sein Leben und Denken,
Herderbücherei 1192, first published 1985 by Verlag Herder,
Freiburg im Breisgau.

© Verlag Herder 1985

Translation © John Bowden 1986

British Library Cataloguing in Publication Data

Vorgrimler, Herbert
Understanding Karl Rahner: an
introduction to his life and thought.
1. Rahner, Karl   2. Catholic Church——
Biography   3. Theologians——Biography
I. Title   II. Kark Rahner verstehen.
English
282'.092'4   BX4705.R287

ISBN 0–334–01723–8

First British edition 1986
by SCM Press Ltd
26-30 Tottenham Road, London N1

Phototypeset by Input Typesetting Ltd
and printed in Great Britain by
Richard Clay (The Chaucer Press) Ltd,
Bungay, Suffolk

Contents

Contents

Preface

'Karl Rahner has renewed the face of our theology. Nothing is quite as it was before him', said Johann Baptist Metz in his fine speech 'Learning and Teaching the Faith. A Thanksgiving to Karl Rahner' (*Den Glauben lernen und lehren. Dank an Karl Rahner*, Munich 1984, 13). He went on: 'Even those who criticize him or reject him still live on his insights, his acute and sensitive perceptions in the world of life and faith.' To a great many people he was more than just a theologian; he was a companion in the faith. Since he said everything about himself that there was to be said, he can continue this role even after his death. The ways which Karl Rahner pointed out and followed have not died with him.

I have written this book for people who ask who Karl Rahner was, and what sort of a man; I was very close to him personally and a friend for more than thirty years. I know what inner drives lay behind his indefatigable work and I think I also know the whole range of his publications. If people are really to be helped to become interested in him, he and his theology cannot be treated in a detached way as 'things'. So I do not want to 'discuss' Karl Rahner but to give an account of him, including personal matters where they show the man more clearly than his writings. Hence I have sometimes also quoted from his many letters to me, and in the Appendix I have included a brief correspondence from the most dramatic period of his life.

Is Karl Rahner really so hard to understand? I believe that this introduction will show that he is easy to understand, but that it is difficult to imitate him, boldly to say 'Nevertheless', as he so often did.

This short book also describes a piece of the history of Christianity in this century, a piece which needs to be remembered in our time as well.

Herbert Vorgrimler

I Approaches and Recollections

1 Experiences of God

This short book is called *Understanding Karl Rahner*. Why is it
sometimes said that the theologian Karl Rahner is so difficult to
understand? There could be two reasons. The first and most
important reason why people do not understand each other is
that one person is not familiar enough with the other, remains
aloof, keeps insights, convictions, experiences to himself or herself
and does not communicate them, in other words does not share
himself or herself with others. The second reason may be that
the person who is so difficult to understand indeed wants to
communicate, but speaks another, incomprehensible language,
for example a specialist language. I shall say something later
about this second reason and therefore about Rahner's specialist
language. The first reason why someone might possibly not be
understood, mentioned above, certainly did not apply to him, for
Karl Rahner was a man who wanted to share the important and
essential things in his life with other people, who confided in
others and sought a way to their hearts. Here I am not referring
primarily to his personal friendships. He was a public figure who
spoke to everyone, who exposed what he wrote to all eyes, and
thus risked incurring criticism for his 'confessions'. For it was said
that those who give away feelings and innermost experiences
prostitute themselves; the personal element has to retreat behind
the subject matter, theology; discretion and silence may be
transcended only in the most intimate group; and as always,
advocates of this attitude may call it 'admirable detachment'.

Karl Rahner had the courage to express himself – his anxieties,
doubt, needs, cares, hopes – and so he discovered among the
many people who saw him, listened to him or read him an
unexpectedly large number who found themselves reflected in

him and in his experiences. He let down his defences and simply trusted them, and this trust was met with reciprocal trust, sympathy and indeed love. I think that it is for this reason, above all, that his writings sold in larger numbers than those of any other theologians and even exceeded the sales of many secular writers, and that this is why right to the end of his life he succeeded in filling rooms with listeners. This was the cause of his following, and not the impetus he gave by providing programmes for the renewal of theology or the reformation of his church. He was a public figure who spoke for himself – and did not, say, hide behind the church as an institution – who wrote about himself and the history of his life with God, and therefore what he kept stressing in interviews in his old age is true: his life and work cannot be separated; he did not lead an interesting life alongside his writing and speaking. He rightly said, 'There is really nothing to be said about me which I have not also written about.'[1]

His is the story of a life with God: this life was centred on the one whom we call 'God'; it was a search for God, a struggle with God, a taking refuge in God, a constant unmasking of idols, a destruction of false images of God, a blind groping for the silent mystery, and yet, sometimes, a joyful immersion in the blessedness of this mystery. All that has been preserved of Karl Rahner tells this story of his life. There is no theological writing in which it has not left traces. However, Karl Rahner's experiences of God are expressed most clearly and in the most comprehensible language in his prayers and meditations; and as there are no experiences of God which are not at the same time experiences of oneself, it is from these writings that the man Karl Rahner emerges most clearly. In language and content, I think that they provide the simplest approach to Karl Rahner, and are the easiest way of understanding him. They contain the key to Karl Rahner the man and the theologian, for they are also theology, in other words an assurance and interpretation of experiences of God. Where prayers were concerned, Rahner himself did not want the reader to feel compelled to pray. He did not write prayers down so that other people should read them to God. He wanted to encourage others, 'his' readers, to express themselves in this or a similar way, to enter into themselves, to discover their innermost depths, to be fully and wholly aware of themselves. and then to find their own words for speaking to God: 'In the last resort it is not a matter of talking *about* prayer, but of the words that we ourselves use to God. And these are words that we must say ourselves. They can be gentle, poor and shy. Like silver doves they can rise to heaven from a joyful heart, or they can be like the inaudible coursing of bitter tears. They can be great and lofty like thunderclaps in the high mountains, or they can be hesitant like the shy confession of a first love. The important thing is that they should come from the heart. If only they *might* come from the heart.'[2] Rahner did not shy away from speaking of the 'heart' – a very important word for him – or of 'silver doves'. He was not concerned with those people who might mock his words as sentimental nonsense, but with people who - understand. This is how Rahner himself wanted his more emotional remarks to be understood: 'People should not be afraid of feelings. The only people who need to be afraid are those without much understanding. The others can be quietly bold enough to be "sentimental", in other words, trust the original impulse of their hearts.'[3]

Useless and lying prayers

Karl Rahner was aware that anyone who tries to pray will inevitably have some expectations in what he or she says to God and that first of all these expectations *must* be disappointed. He often spoke about what prayer cannot achieve, what God cannot bring about in the circumstances of the world. Here two things emerge: an inexorable concern for honesty and considerable experience of life. It was completely alien to Rahner to lull hopeful, seeking or perplexed people to prayer with comforting words, or to envelop real problems of life in a religious mist. Here are two pages from a great deal that could be quoted.

> We have prayed, and God has not answered. We have cried, and he has remained dumb. We have wept tears which have seared our hearts. We were not shown into the presence of his countenance. We could have demonstrated to him that our claims are modest, that they could be fulfilled, seeing that he is the omnipotent one; we could have explained to him that the fulfilment of these petitions is in the deepest interests of his honour in the world and of his kingdom – how else could one still believe that he is the God of righteousness and the Father

of mercy and the God of all comfort, indeed that he exists at all?

We wanted to appeal beyond all reasons and counter-reasons to his heart, to the heart which has mercy and generously commends itself to righteousness and other considerations; we would have had the confidence that moves mountains (if that was all that was lacking); we would have shown him why we already have every reason to be desperate over his silence; we would have produced an endless list of instances: prayer unanswered for starving infants, lamentation unheard for the little ones who suffocate from diphtheria, the grief of raped girls, children beaten to death, slaves exploited in their work, women deceived, those broken by injustice, those who have been 'liquidated', the cripples, the dishonoured; we would have shown him not only our outward distress but our inner torments which do not move God, the torments which have been waiting for an answer since Adam and Eve: Why does the scoundrel prosper and the just person get the worst of it? Why does lightning strike the just and the unjust alike? Why do the fathers sin and the children have to make atonement? Why do lies have such long legs? Why does injustice prosper so well? Why is world history one long stream of foolishness, meanness and brutality?

And we would have sworn to him after these questions: by your honour, by your glory, by your name in this world, which one day you must defend, help us to find slightly clearer traces of you in this comfortless world: traces of your wisdom, your justice and your goodness. But please, we would have gone on to say, we want to experience your help in such a way that people cannot say that such help would be inevitable, even if there were no God, so that nobody can say that everyone has a certain number of wins in the lifelong lottery of this world, whether or not he or she prays beforehand, and therefore there is no need to attribute a few pieces of good luck to the power of prayer. We would have called to his Son, who knows what it is like to be human because he has shared our life. We could have done all that. We would have done all that – we certainly would. For we *have* prayed. We have begged. We have sent glowing, evocative words heavenwards. And it has been no use. We have just wept like children who know that in the end the policeman takes the lost ones home. But no one came to wipe *our* tears from our eyes and comfort us. We prayed, but we were not heard. We called, but no answer came. We cried, but everything remained so silent that in the end our crying would just have seemed ridiculous had we not been oppressed by distress and despair.[4]

How many people will have had precisely those experiences of God before 1946, when Rahner wrote these words, and from then down to the present? We can see from this text how honestly Rahner analyses a situation. And then, unlike other critics of religion, he does not put faith, religion and prayer aside, but inexorably goes on asking questions, because 'behind' the manifold human failures there is not nothing, but the beginning of the dark mystery of men which touches on God. However, at the same time, honest analyses like these obviously, inevitably, offended, provoked or unsettled the 'pious', who thought they knew so much about God and his ways, those in search of miracles, and a number of representatives of the church. A fundamentally compassionate man like Rahner did not want to provoke for the sake of provocation, but for God's sake. Because the one who can be possessed and controlled, the one who can be seen through and planned for, is not God.

Rahner sought to reach yet another group of people, to unsettle them and if possible to shake them: the middle-class citizens who as it were practise religion on the side, in a lukewarm and half-hearted way, with the feeling that it is not very important but that in the end there might be something in it.

There are human affairs, actions of the heart, which everyone thinks he knows because everyone talks about them, because they are evidently very simple. But the most natural and simplest actions of the heart are the most difficult, and people learn them only slowly. And if they knew them at the end of their lives, their lives were good, precious and blessed. These actions of the heart, which are at the same time the easiest and the most difficult, include goodness, unselfishness, love, silence, understanding, true joy – and prayer. No, it really is not easy to know and understand what prayer is. Perhaps people were once aware of it or knew it at a time when their poor hearts were not yet so worn by bitterness and the joys of life, when they were perhaps capable of pure love. But then something else happens without their noticing – just as love can become habit and perhaps a two-person egoism – though they still think that they are praying. Then they either give up, disappointed and bored, because they slowly realize that what they are trying to do is no longer worth the effort. Or they go on 'praying' (if you can call what they are doing 'prayer') and it's like going to a government office: you either have a bill to pay or an allowance to receive, and so they go there in God's name. They need something from God and so they ask for it; they don't want to incur his displeasure, and so they do their duty; to some extent they pay their respects to him (not too long; what has to be said is soon said, and surely he too will see that we don't have much time and have more important things to do). And this visit to the highest office in the world (one has the impression that he hears an enormous number of petitions and functions in a very mediocre way) and these official respects paid to the supreme Governor of the world, in order not to fall out of favour (because at all events that could be dangerous after death – one never knows), is called prayer. O God, that is not prayer, but the shell of prayer, a cheat.[5]

Disillusionment over the false God

And so, just as such prayers are only the shell of prayer, a cheat, in the same way much faith is only a shell and a cheat, and so too are some ideas of God. According to Rahner, the insight that much in some religion is dead bears within it the germ of new life. This insight, and the work of clearing away which goes with it, is painful. And no one can be certain whether he or she has done this work once and for all in life. New illusions about God, other false images of God, appear unexpectedly – and in turn are doomed to destruction. Thus even in his old age Karl Rahner could say that he too was threatened by atheism, and so he could think himself into the minds of various figures of atheism, trace the inner reasoning and motivation which lead to a rejection of faith. Here we find a very important feature of his theological thought. There are no clear dividing lines anywhere, and when it comes to God and the questions of religion and faith it is impossible to distingush clear blocks of good and evil. Truth and error are not related like black and white. In a good deal of what official Christianity regards as error there gleams the tiny flame of truth which no one quenches unscathed. Rahner's thought is not exclusive, but inclusive and comprehensive. And one of the elements which holds believers together with so many who regard themselves as atheists is to be found in the hiddenness and permanent incomprehensibility of God:

> They say that there is no God because they confuse the true God with the one whom they regarded as their God. And they are right in what they really think. The God whom they thought to be God really does not exist: the God of earthly security, the God of deliverance from the disappointments of life, the God who provides assurance for life, the God who sees to it that children do not cry and that justice comes down on earth to transform the grief of the earth, the God who will not allow human love to end in disappointment.[6]

Karl Rahner's life was lived in the tension between the disappointment of false ideas of God and the longing for the true God, and clarity did not increase with increasing old age. Johann Baptist Metz has described the religion of Karl Rahner in an attractive passage: Rahner did not live in the familiar homeland of a middle-class religion, with a feeling of certainty and security; he did not have a kind of optimism about God. Rather, his religion was like the silent sigh of creation, a wordless cry before the veiled countenance of God, a leaden longing, an unprotected homelessness. This basic mood became even more oppressive in his old age – though Rahner made great efforts to overcome it 'because the road is not at an end and he is very weary; because too many ashes already cover the dim glow of life and no wind from paradise rekindles them; because an insidious feeling of superfluity can bring out all the difficulties of this longing for God...'.[7]

Love

In his religious texts Karl Rahner did not just express his disappointments over God and his longing for God; he also revealed a heart devoted to humanity. I would like to demonstrate that from just two examples, two important themes which could easily be multiplied. These are the themes of love and anger. Karl Rahner was a loving man. By that I do not simply mean that he entertained loving feelings and extended them to others. I mean that he gave others a firm, inalienable place in his heart and that he always tried to make the greatest contribution that love can make: to recognize the person one loves *as* the other, who does not think in the same way and does not have the same desires, and in that way not to imprison him or her under an obligation (however well meant), making them a possession, but leaving them free.

He often spoke of love, not just in a general and abstract way, but of his own love, and he once commented in a troubled way:'How anxious we are to ensure that nothing of the love which we entertain in our hearts shall be noticed![8] Although he left room for feelings, and love was certainly an emotional matter as far as he was concerned, he stressed just as strongly, indeed even more strongly, another element of love which is completely accessible to the impulses of the will, namely fidelity. He was aware of the excessively high percentage of failed relationships, partnerships and marriages, and yet continually hoped to find successful love, which meant constant faithfulness – which is not imprisonment or just going through the motions. He always believed that miracles were possible in the sphere of love. He spoke of love and fidelity in the text of a prayer in which he remembered his own dead before God:

> The real course of my life, formed by those who love, will become increasingly smaller and more silent, until I too silently leave the way and depart without farewell or return.
>
> Therefore my heart is with those who have already taken this way before me. There is no substitute for them; there are no other people who can fill up the number of a group who really love one another, once one of them is suddenly and unexpectedly no longer there. For no one can replace the other in true love. For true love loves the other to such a depth that each individual is only himself or herself. Therefore each of those who have gone hence has taken something of my heart with them, indeed often my whole heart, when death has gone through my life. Anyone who has really loved and still loves finds life changed, even before death, into a living with the dead. For could the one who loves forget his or her dead? And if someone has really loved, then his 'forgetting' and 'having exhausted his tears' is

not the sign of being comforted again, but of the ultimacy of his mourning, the sign that a piece of his own heart has really died with the dead person and now is living dead, and *therefore* can no longer weep.[9]

For Karl Rahner, love is a power which changes people, inexplicably takes them beyond themselves, and thus reveals something quite mysterious. However, it does not lead a person to lose himself or herself; on the contrary, it is a form in which a person first finds himself or herself fulfilled. Love means sharing, sharing with others; that was a basic need of Rahner's. He was not a solitary person. In human terms he lived from the strength which arises from a very small number of people who completely trust one another. He once used the Old Testament phrase 'a stout shelter', one which gives support and security in life,[10] to describe this inner circle. He lived by friendships which by the nature of things could not be great in number. From this inner circle he received a good deal of the confidence with which he could address a wider audience and readership, and be there for others. For Karl Rahner, being there for others meant being lavish with his small amount of time, finding time for others, not giving himself much holiday, taking on commitments, being inventive in his search for help of a quite specific kind, having civil courage, indeed adopting public stances, even at the risk of losing sympathizers. We shall be discussing that later. At all events Rahner understood love not just as a matter of feelings and assertions, but as an energy which always needed to be proved in praxis – including political praxis. For Karl Rahner love had its supreme form in practical selflessness (which he never identified with loss of the ego). Karl Rahner was always amazed at people who were able to live in a virtually selfless way. Thus for example a young woman called Andrea even found a place in one of his prayers because 'for a whole year during her studies, without charge she did the washing for young delinquents in a home'.[11]

Anger

From there it is easy to speak about Karl Rahner's anger. He was a peace-loving person who in essentials avoided conflicts. Above all, when he himself was the object, he could put up with injustice for a long time without challenging it. He barely defended himself against theological attacks. Even when other people misbehaved grossly, he looked for excuses or at least for explanations of their actions. However, he became vehement and angry when people put forward exalted principles and even called themselves 'God's representatives' ('to tell the truth, I don't like the word because God cannot be represented')[12] and required love from others without themselves living by it. He often encountered this attitude among church officials who had ceased to recognize human sensibilities and feelings of sympathy, but rather subordinated love to the supposed interests of their position. When that happened Karl Rahner became angry, even in prayer:

> How tedious, senile, just concerned for the reputation of the apparatus, how short-sighted, how domineering those who 'hold office' in the church seem to me to be! In a bad sense they are conservative and clerical. And when they become unctuous, when they blatantly display their goodwill and their unselfishness, it gets even worse, because I can hardly bear to listen to them confessing their mistakes and failings publicly and clearly. They want us to believe in their infallibility and forget the major blunders and omissions of which they were guilty yesterday. I find it more difficult to detect how often have they been in righteous indignation over a specificic action: holy anger over a social order which is an ultimate cause. They moralize a great deal, but often one cannot see so much of the transports of joy at the message of grace which fills spirit and heart to bursting point, and in which you give your whole self. Yet their moral preaching would have much more chance of being heard if it were a brief passing comment in this joyful praise of your glorious grace, the abundance of life that you want to give us.[13]

I shall be talking later about Karl Rahner's relation to the church, which is what this angry comment addressed to God is about. The two examples of love and anger may be enough support for what I said earlier. Karl Rahner the human being expresses himself in his prayers, with his disappointments and longings, with his theology, with his human heart in which there was love and from which anger could arise. The prayers are therefore an appropriate approach to Karl Rahner.

The primal experience

Anyone who goes on to ask more questions about how to approach the theology of Karl Rahner should not overlook the fact that this theology has a quite personal, deeply rooted basis, the experience of God himself:

> I have experienced God directly. I have experienced God, the nameless and unfathomable one, the one who is silent and yet near, in the trinity of his approach to me. I have really encountered God, the true and living one, the one for whom this name that quenches all names is fitting. God himself. I have experienced God himself, not human words about him. This experience is not barred to anyone. I want to communicate it to others as well as I can.[14]

It was in statements of this kind that the aged Karl Rahner spoke about the primal experience which completely captivated him while he was still young and which provides the key to his life and work. This experience of God was so completely sure and clear to him that he could say that it had led to such certainty of faith that his faith would remain unshaken even if the basic document of Christian faith, Holy Scripture, did not exist.[15] At the same time he insisted that this experience of God was not at all extraordinary nor accessible only to the privileged. The experience of God happens to anyone, as to Karl Rahner, in the midst of specific, ordinary everyday experiences, in particular events in which people suddenly find themselves torn away from dealing with quite ordinary matters and tasks and thrown back on themselves; they can no longer escape, yet feel an inward motive force which comes from elsewhere, supporting and urging on.

In any life there are events of this kind which have an inner nucleus:

> Thus it is when man is suddenly reduced to a state of '*aloneness*', when every individual thing recedes, as it were, into remoteness and silence and disappears in this, when everything is 'called in question', as we are accustomed to say, when the silence resounds more penetratingly than the accustomed din of everyday life.
> Thus it is when man suddenly experiences that he is inescap-

ably brought face to face with his own freedom and *responsibility*, feeling this as a single and total factor embracing the whole of his life and leaving him no further refuge, no possibility of acquittal from guilt. Thus it is in those cases in which man can no longer find any approval or support, can no longer hope for any recognition or any thanks, in which he finds himself called to account for his actions to that silent and infinite reality which is not ours to shape or control, which exists and is not subject to us, that which is most interior to us and most different from us at the same time. Thus it is when man experiences how this reality silently extends itself, as it were, throughout the whole of existence, permeating everything, unifying everything, while remaining itself incomprehensible...is still present in the form of judgement even when we deny that we are answerable to it and seek to escape from it

Thus it is when man suddenly makes the experience of personal *love* and encounter, suddenly notices, startled and blessed in this both at once, the fact that he has been accepted with a love which is absolute and unconditional even though, when he considers himself alone in all his finitude and frailty, he can assign no reason whatever, find no adequate justification, for this unconditional love that reaches out to him from the other side. Thus it is too when man experiences the fact that he himself likewise loves – loves with an inconceivable audacity that overcomes the questionability of the other even though he is aware of this, when he experiences that this love of his is so absolute that it commits him to finding support in a reality which is no longer subject to his control, which is most interior to the love itself in its inconceivability and yet at the same time is different from it.

Thus it is when *death* silently directs its gaze towards a man – that death which causes all to fall into its own nothingness and precisely in doing this, provided only that it is willingly accepted (thus and only thus), does not strike man dead but itself transforms him, liberates him, endows him with that freedom which no longer appeals to or finds support in anything beyond itself, and yet at the same time is unconditional.

This is a line of thought which we could and should follow further so as to point out how this single basic experience of man is present in a thousand different forms, and in this experience it is borne in upon him that his existence is open to the inconceivable mystery. In it he remarks that he is the prisoner of his own terrifying finitude (which does exist, and which cruelly torments him) only so long as he turns his eyes away from the infinitude and inconceivable reality which encompasses him on every side, or when he shrinks from it in terror because its power silently and uncontrollably pervades all.

It is at this level that we should speak of joy, of faithfulness, of the ultimate *Angst* to which man is subject, of the yearning which transcends every individual reality, of the fear which we feel at the inexorability of truth – that truth which is still there even when it is denied or mocked at. This is the level at which we should speak of the peace that comes from that detachment which never clings onto any individual reality in the absolute, and so gains all of the experience of the beautiful which is the assured promise of that which still lies in the future, of the experience of that radical and inescapable guilt which is nevertheless suddenly and inconceivably forgiven. This is the level at which we should speak of our experience of the fact that that which seems simply to belong to the past nevertheless in truth having come to be, *is* and in a true and sacred sense is still in force. This is the level at which we should speak of our experience of the infinite openness of the future which is inexhaustible promise.

We might proceed still further along this line of thought, and our vision would have to become far more concrete still – concrete not in the sense that it would cause us to lose ourselves in the particular realities of the external world, but rather in the sheer density of that experience which is ultimate and yet present at the same time everywhere in our everyday lives, for in these man is forever occupied with the grains of sand along the shore where he dwells at the edge of the infinite ocean of mystery.[16]

Is that a 'difficult' text which hinders rather than helps access to Rahner? I do not think so. It simply has to be read slowly and meditated on. Life is full of events which have a mysterious nucleus. Taken by itself, a single event may not prove much: perhaps a single experience of solitude, of responsibility - a responsibility, for example, which suddenly dawns on one as the inner voice of conscience, to make peace, to reject war and military service, a claim which is not supported by the approval of relatives or people around, which does not allow any escape, which intervenes in the whole of life and changes it -, a single experience of love or death. Taken by itself, one experience could only say a 'little'; it could be interpreted in different ways. But as Rahner says, there are a thousand such experiences in a human life – and underlying them all is the one primal experience: that man is more than the sum of chemical elements and processes, that human life rests on an incomprehensible mystery, indeed constantly begins to flow in that direction.

This is no daydream born of the infinite longings of humanity. For daydreams come from what is already understood and reach out towards something which is already known in some way. The mystery of humanity, in humanity, is precisely that which is not understood and is incomprehensible. For example, it happens in love, when a person must say, 'I myself, limited as I am, fragmentary and unreliable as I am, *cannot* be the ground for the unconditional love that another person has towards me'; and: 'I myself am well aware how questionable the beloved person is, and at the same time – in a way which I cannot understand – I feel in myself a boldness which goes beyond the limits of the other person.' On both occasions love is absolute: it rests and lives on a foundation which does not lie only in the one who loves, and cannot be guided and governed by him or her. It is – incomprehensible. And this is the experience of God.

Human greatness

Why did Rahner inwardly and formally feel the urge to disclose to others these possibilities of experiencing God in the everyday? Why should someone who is completely occupied with the grains of sand along the shore lift up his eyes and see that he is dwelling on the shore of an infinite sea? Because, Rahner replies, someone who does not recognize the innermost nearness of the incomprehensible mystery or at least have intimations of it does not know himself. He does not grasp his own greatness and significance, the call of an infinite mystery, and therefore is threatened by the danger of failing to recognize the true magnitude and significance of his fellow human beings – in whom alone this infinite mystery dwells. Not to have such self-knowledge would go against the innermost tendency of every human being. Everyone must know who he or she ultimately is. Moreover it would also go against the ultimate determination of humanity. For its way into the incomprehensible mystery is a way into that which is truly unbounded: to remain once and for all in the presence of the infinite mystery is the meaning of every human life. But not to think of people in this way would also have immediate political and social consequences. Wherever this ultimate greatness and destiny of the individual is not seen and acknowledged, there is a danger that an individual may be eliminated as being not productive enough, not important and valuable enough, unusable and useless; or that a still 'usable' person may be 'used' as mere material for 'higher' ends, for example a happier future.

Karl Rahner did not attempt to operate with threats and intimidation in order to make people see; he did not spell out what happens to a human being who does not enquire into his or her own deepest mystery. Rather, in constantly new ways he sought to show that in the process of a life a human being 'makes' something of himself or herself which will remain for ever – because no one, not even God, can undo what human beings have done in freedom: they acquire a form, a profile, a format in which they will be God's partner for eternity. Every human being makes himself something that he entrusts to God for ever.

Because these are the ultimate and most important questions of human life, as Johann Baptist Metz rightly says,[17] Karl Rahner invites his hearers and readers on a voyage of discovery in hardly known areas of their own lives, where they too are not afraid to look into the abyss. And his life work was one long rebellion against the lack of mystery in our time, against the inability to mourn and be comforted; a struggle against the often anonymous manipulators and deceivers who promise people that they will be free of desire and suffering and happy in the fulfilment of their needs, and therefore be content with themselves and their banality. Rahner sought to protect people from this 'misfortune without desire'.

Uncertainty and decision

Karl Rahner did not raise these questions in a timeless context. He was constantly concerned afresh with the difficulties of perceiving God and believing in God under the conditions of 'modern times'. He knew that the truth of faith can no longer be demonstrated in the old, naive way. The 'desacralizing' of the cosmos, the control of the world by science and technology, have meant that we no longer encounter mystery in nature. God's rule of the world does not express itself in a divine intervention in the history of the world. Rahner did not feel the disappearance of the old, 'popular' faith to be tragic; he saw here a decline of superstition and at the same time new opportunities. He was convinced that today the mystery of man's own nature emerges all the more clearly. One simply has to ask deeply enough and describe clearly enough what emerges from the question itself.

Rahner did not condemn people who do not perceive this, their innermost mystery. He looked for excuses for people, although he knew that really guilty refusal – hidden to others, and accessible only to God – can blind the eyes. He demonstrated that people are very well aware of their innermost mystery, their inner voice, but sometimes in circumstances which Christians cannot interpret. He stressed that the true God can be affirmed even in the negation of a supposed God. And he stressed above all and always: 'Love of the neighbour is the primary act of the love of God.'[18]

He also saw that the reasons advanced from the theological side for recognizing the infinite mystery and trusting in it cannot be presented with certainty and clarity on all sides. There are no proofs to help on the way to God. There is only a multiplicity of insights, intimations and abysses, which lure people to let go and leap – without the certainty of a safe landing. Rahner saw this situation of the person asking and seeking God as the context of a decision: it is the honour and responsibility of humanity, since we are not forced to God, though we are responsible if we avoid a decision. Rahner sought to encourage such people to a tranquil and bold decision: no one need deny himself, his doubt, or his negative experiences; the yes to the divine mystery happens to a large degree *against* appearances, but it is nevertheless, nevertheless, meaningful and honest, since it embraces greater human possibiities than scepticism and doubt could.

Rahner sees an indispensable support to this bold yes to the divine mystery in Jesus of Nazareth. In him the experiences of God, the intimations of his nearness, the longings for ultimate meaning find confirmation: in his life, in the way in which he endured his death, and in the experience that God did not abandon him in death.

Here I would like to draw attention to an important approach to Karl Rahner's theology which is not by way of his (academic) christology but by his piety focussed on Jesus. I mean first of all his meditations on the passion and death of Jesus. They frame and accompany his publications, beginning from 'Holy Hour and Commemoration of the Passion' (*Heilige Stunde und Passionsandacht*), a short mystical writing which was published for the first time in 1949 under the pseudonym Anselm Trescher (Trescher was his mother's maiden name) and which later was often reprinted under his name with the title 'Words on the Cross' (*Worte vom Kreuz*), to his contribution to Anita Röper's book *Stationen*, 1978. The God whom from everyday experiences we suspect to be the deepest mystery of human life here assumes in our history the particular human countenance of love which shares in suffering.

Karl Rahner did not enjoy great and solemn liturgies, but he attached a great deal of importance to the 'silent' mass. For him it was a place of complete concentration. He looked for ways of keeping it free from disturbances and distractions. In his first period at Innsbruck he got up at five in the morning to celebrate the eucharist completely alone. I can remember walking with him to mountain churches (Höttinger Bild, St Georgenberg) in the Tyrol which promised tranquillity and loneliness for this celebration. Karl Rahner did not want to keep secret what he felt from God on such occasions; he did not regard even the most private experience as a private possession. Among his many publications from the early period down to the last years of his life there are meditations with the title 'eucharistic worship' ('Eucharistische Anbetung').

As often as Karl Rahner looked into the history of humanity or even into individual human careers he was filled with sorrow and even pessimism. The world of brutalities, the camps, the holocaust, institutional violence and oppression were not left out of his work or suppressed, and in the private sphere he experienced too much betrayal, lack of trust and failure to be able to set much store by human achievements. But as soon as he looked on the outcome of history as a whole and at individual human destiny he was remarkable optimistic. The beginning and end of each and every human life is caught up into the unspeakable nearness of the divine mystery and hidden in it. From here there comes into Karl Rahner's theological words a confidence which has comforted and strengthened many people in oppression and anxiety, but has also come incurred vigorous protest from others. Rahner thought so radically about the incomprehensible divine mystery that the worst he could imagine was not this or that man-made catastrophe, but more profoundly the forgetting of this mystery. But even that left him unshaken:

> Will there ever be people who no longer have any ear for the word of God in principle, and in all phases of their existence? Will there ever be people who no longer enquire beyond the endless variety of questions that can be asked over this and that into what cannot be said? Will there ever be people who always and with real success forbid themselves to allow the approach of ultimate mystery, which governs their being namelessly as its ultimate ground and ultimate goal; that allows us to say 'You' in love, that makes us fall into its abyss so that we can be free? What if that were possible and became reality?
>
> That sort of thing could not shake me. In that case human beings would have reverted as individuals or as humanity to inventive animals, and the human history of freedom, responsibility, guilt and forgiveness would be at an end. But this would only have changed the nature of the end that we Christians expect anyway. Human beings really worthy of this name would have found eternal life.[19]

2   Servant of the Word

'I have always done theology for the sake of proclamation, of preaching, of pastoral care.'[20] This remark by Karl Rahner first

of all means that he understood himself as the servant of those
who had undertaken ministry to their fellow human beings by
communicating to them the word of God as it is contained in the
Christian tradition. These official and semi-official ministers, men
and women, need a great deal of help in understanding the old
sacred texts and bringing them up to date. However, Karl Rahner
felt an even deeper commitment to the word of God: he himself
preached in different ways, by word of mouth and in writing.
Here I would like to mention the most important forms of his
ministry of the word.

Karl Rahner himself often preached, addressed people in
religious, liturgical contexts. He preached in large churches to
many people: in St Michael's Church, Munich during Lent 1946,
in the Minster at Freiburg (e.g. in the student mission of December
1951) and in the Cathedral at Münster. He also preached to a few
people in small chapels, at weddings, at first masses, at the jubilees
of ordination to the priesthood or entering an Order. He preached
for ten years in Innsbruck, mostly in the Spitalkirche, as the Jesuit
church was still destroyed. In Innsbruck some of his sermons were
taken down in writing by his hearers; in 1965 I edited a collection
under the title *Biblical Homilies* (an English translation was
published in 1966), and at Rahner's request wrote a preface for
them. He himself prepared other sermons in written form and
could therefore later include them in his spiritual writings.[21]

The same can be said of these sermons as of Rahner's prayers.
They represent an authentic approach to Rahner's theology in
easier language, though their content is not 'cheaper' – and also
to Rahner the man.

One of Rahner's special services to pastoral care and the
ministry of the word is his Exercises, based on the *Spiritual
Exercises* by Ignatius of Loyola, the founder of the Jesuits. The
Exercises of Ignatius are to be distinguished from other important
and meaningful spiritual exercises. They are not a theological
course with a religious slant, nor extended 'days of penitence'.
Nor are they a course in group dynamics or the like with a
Christian stamp, or meditation exercises aimed at acquiring inner
tranquillity and recollection, facilitating one's penetration of
deeper personal depths and dimensions, the kind of thing that has
again become topical above all under the stimulus of the Far East.
'Real spiritual exercises are the serious attempt, following a

certain plan, to make a definite decision or choice at a decisive point in time... a decision such as this is received from God and from his grace alone.'[22] It is lengthy perseverance in an ultimate solitude in which a person breaks through, beyond all words and concepts, to God – God himself. 'The director of the Exercises does not communicate from the ultimate nature of these exercises the official word of the church as such, deeply rooted though they may be in the church. Rather, he simply gives help (when he can), cautiously and from afar, help so that God and human beings really encounter one another directly.'[23] Karl Rahner often directed Exercises during his life, right down to the last year of his life. A text of his meditations, which he presented in the form of a week's Exercises, was published.[24] In a conversation about 'the direct experience of God in the Exercises', in 1978, he expressed the conviction that Ignatian Exercises today have a greater significance than ever. For today the social aids to religion are dying out, and not even the usual aids of a church kind, not even the sacraments, can keep alive a real relationship with God. Rahner is convinced that this relationship remains alive 'only through a last direct encounter of the human being with God' of a kind which the Exercises can communicate and which, by Rahner's own testimony, have indeed communicated to him.[25]

The theologian

In this section I want to try to give a summary account of Karl Rahner the theologian without at this stage going into the details of his work. He wanted to put his life as a theologian always at the service of fellow human beings and the word of God and never do theology for theology's sake.

Rahner took the study of theology seriously. He read and taught intensively, following a fixed programme. Of course there were focal points within the context of such a study. Karl Rahner began from the experiences that he had had in the Ignatian Exercises,[26] and in a series of historical investigations applied himself to the roots of this piety; however, he did not want to become a historian. In the years in which he began to teach he continued intensive theological study, and in so doing laid the foundations for his lifelong activity as professor of dogmatics. His philosophical study, with Thomas Aquinas as its focal point, had theological relevance. Karl Rahner acquired an extraordinary capacity for concentrated reading and training his memory. After the long years of study he had an enormous knowledge. The content extended from the Bible, which he had worked through often with the help of exegetical commentaries, through the theological tradition of the church fathers, the scholars of the Middle Ages and the baroque period to theologians – of course, selected theologians – of the two great confessions of the twentieth century. From this wealth of knowledge, to the end of his life he could cite examples, arguments and also deterrent patterns of behaviour. He had become a theological specialist through and through, also with specialist knowledge in the history of theology, relating to the group of problems connected with grace, sin, repentance and penance. This gave him a great respect for professional theological specialist work, in particular for research into the history of dogmas, especially when it was made to have a bearing on the present. We may not forget that he produced new editions of Denziger, the scholarly collection of church dogmas and other supreme statements of doctrine in Latin, from the 28th to the 31st editions inclusively, and that from the second edition of 1948 until his death he supervised the German-language edition of church doctrinal texts, Neuner-Roos, in later years supported by his pupil Karl-Heinz Weger. It would be a fundamental misunderstanding of Karl Rahner to see him only as a mystic, a charismatic or one who provided stimuli. The extensive content of his knowledge was the indispensable basis for his ability to speak with knowledge of the subject, with an authority which came from within.

However, all that has been said so far could equally well have been said of other theologians. This is not what makes Rahner's theological style unmistakable. Johann Baptist Metz seems to me to have given the best possible description of Karl Rahner's character as a theologian:[27] the basic feature of Rahner's theology is not criticism but rescue. Rahner wanted to rescue the abiding and, in his view, indispensable elements in the content of the church's doctrine of faith. Here he attempted, successfully, to uncover the overgrown and suppressed insights and aims of traditional scholastic theology, the inner dynamic which was hidden even from itself, in order to release new fruitfulness. He set to work on this task by seeking with all the strength at his disposal, to do away with the division between doctrine and life, between theological system and religious experience. Metz rightly criticizes scholastic theology, and above all the doctrine of faith, dogmatics, for often acting 'as a phobia which has been turned into a system directed against life that it does not understand'.[28] Rahner seeks to overcome this phobia with the power of creative mediation. Here, turning the whole knowledge of the system upside down, he begins with the questions posed by life itself. And in this way the subject – which has questions, which may ask questions – is elevated into the dogmatic awareness of scholastic theology.[29]

This emergence of the questioning subject, this starting point in human questions, both of which are characteristic of Rahner, has been called the 'anthropocentric shift' in theology. Sometimes regrets have been expressed about it, as though here God no longer holds first place in theology. Rahner has called such playing off of man against God and thus the charges against his theology 'absolute nonsense':[30]

> How can a Christian speak appropriately of God unless at the same time he also speaks of man? The word made flesh is and remains the eternal and unlimited man. We cannot know God as he is without at the same time thinking of him as the God who made man. Consequently we cannot have a complete theology without considering its anthropological aspects. If we want to talk of God properly, we have to talk of human beings.[31]

But which human beings? Who is the subject for whom Rahner has found a place in scholastic theology? Rahner tends to speak of 'man' in in a timeless and unworldly way. The question who is meant by this has been studied more closely in the theology which has come into being after Rahner, though it is inconceivable without him. The man in Rahner's theology who investigates the theological heritage is not a brilliant, interesting personality but the average middle-class person from central Europe, the person Rahner understood himself to be. Metz aptly remarks: 'Rahner's theology is the dogmatics of the ordinary, dare I say average, Christian concerned with the history of his life – the mystical biography of an undramatic life without great changes and conversions.'[32] In it is expressed not the climactic experience of a visionary (who with his spiritual eye penetrates into the life of the deity, as this is reported by some women and some men in the Christian tradition), but the 'collective routine experience of the Catholic'.[33] It is precisely for that reason that he could be important for so many people, because they felt that he understood them, because they saw how he took up their questions - which sometimes they did not even understand themselves – and helped to sort them out.

The Protestant theologian Wolfhart Pannenberg expresses the same sentiments when he says that Karl Rahner is a Roman Catholic theologian through and through and yet that in every question, however specialized, his thought culminates in humanity as a whole; he makes the Christian element become transparent to humanity generally, and people felt that their questions were part of Rahner's experience.[34]

Metz has found words which get to the heart of things, which characterize the theologian and the man Karl Rahner quite generally: 'Rahner has an almost proletarian antipathy to anything that is élitist and esoteric.'[35] It would be élitist theological behaviour simply to pass over people's questions and needs and speak of God as though God were important only for himself. It would be esoteric to speak of the nature and the will of God in the garb of an initiate, to practise theology as secret knowledge. When Rahner was disturbed and impelled by an innermost impulse of conscience to speak theologically in such a way that his words could 'reach' fellow human beings, this was not mere adaptation, adjusting the word of God to human standards; it was taking people seriously by noting the way in which God himself took humanity seriously.

From his own experience there arose the basic theological conviction that God has revealed himself to *every* human being and that this is the authentic and most original form of revelation. Therefore it does not need special bearers of the mystery who control it; rather, sometimes it needs a kind of midwife, since not all human beings are in a position to understand and interpret their lives, and what happens to them. For Rahner it was the will of God himself that human beings should learn to interpret their experiences of God in the way that the Jewish-Christian tradition of God interpreted them.

After his programmed period of theological development Rahner no longer himself sought out the theological themes on which he wanted to say something; he no longer set out to investigate an unexplored area of the past and make it fruitful for the present. As Metz puts it very well, 'he was not simply interested in the interesting but felt himself obligated by the needs, the questions of others', and in so doing showed himself to be a master in the art of bringing questions to birth.[36] Hence the remarkable literary form of his work.

The title of the series in which many of his writings are collected is *Schriften zur Theologie* ('Writings on Theology': in the English translation this became *Explorations in Theology*). He preferred to see himself as a dilettante in comparison with the guild of learned theologians. And he spoke without false regard for his reputation and the sensibilities of colleagues in respect of questions from the sphere of theological disciplines which were not his own. He wrote articles on fundamental theology, practical theology and moral theology, and yet was at home 'only' as a dogmatic theologian and historian of dogma. In a letter to me on 22 November 1961 he made a telling remark: 'And particularly (excuse my fancy) anyone who has learned anything from me should not take the question of specialism too seriously. Today I would still be ready to change to moral theology, or to pastoral theology.' My fellow-students at Innsbruck, Helmut Erharter and Wilhelm Zauner, aptly wrote in a 'Thank-you to Karl Rahner':

> His speciality at the university was dogmatics. But his students knew that one could also learn philosophy, exegesis and moral theology from him, indeed everything that a theological faculty has to offer. When it came to detailed information he often referred us to his colleagues, but it always sounded rather special when one of these referred to him as "my colleague". Rahner did not fit into a specialism, into the system of theological disciplines; the format was too large. Therefore some people also found him disturbing when their format fitted exactly into the discipline.[37]

Difficult language

But how did it come about on the one hand that here was a theologian who sought to communicate the truth of faith to people of today by taking up their questions, who shared their anxieties and needs, unconcerned whether he was a professional specialist or not, and on the other that the academic language which this theologian spoke was felt by many people to be so difficult? Indeed, one can often hear the view that Rahner is impossible to understand.

One preliminary remark. There is also a history to Rahner's language. In his old age his language was simpler, plainer, looser; the sentences were shorter. The reason for this was not only that he had heard the numerous complaints about his language and was ready to correct himself wherever a change of opinion did not go against his conscience. Nor did he any longer have the feeling that he had to use countless subordinate clauses to safeguard himself against the suspicion that what he said was incompatible with church tradition. And he had had to note that 'the' philosophy with which his language was initially stamped no longer existed. These are already some reasons why many people found the language of his earlier articles so overloaded.

The early Karl Rahner addressed above all the 'educated' among puzzled Christians and searching non-believers: academics, people with school-leaving qualifications, like those who joined in the Salzburg High School Weeks of 1937. He wanted to speak to them in the language of the philosophically educated of that time, in the language of Heidegger, Jaspers, the Christian 'personalists' (though here again there were limits to his enterprise). But Rahner was also profoundly moulded by the language of his church, Latin. Like so many even of his earliest pupils he had heard all his lectures in Latin and had to challenge the disputations which went with them in spontaneous Latin. He had taught Latin himself for a long time. Then he gave lectures in Latin on the basis of Latin manuscripts. He conversed in Latin with foreign theological visitors, even with the French, whose language he could speak. He spoke Latin with John XXIII and Paul VI and wrote letters in the language even in the year he died. How could something that was so deeply rooted not shape his language?

Karl Rahner's academic theological language is characterized by the attempt to express the truth that he recognized with the help of all the possibilities of syntax, above all with participles, which are otherwise rarely used in German. He did this in such a way that in the end old terms which otherwise were only repeated formally finally themselves conveyed the 'substance' and were not devalued as a result. That means that such attempts by Rahner at the same time include the sum of previous theological insights, packed into subsidiary clauses with 'if' and 'in so far as' and into countless participles. It does not escape those who know the subjects concerned that this 'inclusion' presupposes great historical and systematic knowledge and also serves to guarantee the orthodoxy of the statement. As an example I would like to quote a single long sentence in which Rahner describes the Catholic understanding of grace and nature:

> Grace is the *a priori* capacity for the co-natural acceptance of the self-disclosure of God in the word (faith – love) and in the beatific vision; nature is the abiding constitution of man presupposed in this ability to hear which is of such a kind that the sinner and unbeliever can shut himself off from this impelling self-disclosure of God without implicitly affirming again what is negated in this No (as in the guilty No to his metaphysical being) and in such a way that this self-disclosure can appear to the human being, as one who is already created, as the free miracle of personal love that he cannot require of himself (= 'nature'), although it can be promised to him and he is essentially open to it (nature as positive *potentia oboedientialis* for supernatural grace).[38]

Such a sentence contains the whole teaching of the church's tradition about the relationship of grace and nature along with the classical understanding of these two entities. Rahner's own formulations – 'self-disclosure of God', 'free miracle of personal love' – may strike the reader directly. Of course such a statement is not simple; nor is it the product of the self-importance of its author. Rahner began by presupposing a reader who wants to invest goodwill and energy in reading and not consume the text in a superficial way. Towards the end of his life he became aware that there were fewer and fewer such readers, just as there were neither theological students nor professors nor bishops who could converse in Latin without difficulty and fluently. He had often been preoccupied with the question how what had been conceived of formerly and down to the present day could nevertheless be preserved because it contains important elements which are valuable to the tradition, and also because without the handing on of tradition in this way Christianity runs the risk of losing its identity.

Rahner was convinced that only such a basis – knowledge of the tradition *and* awareness of the possibilities which are concealed in it – gives one the right to offer loyal criticism of church statements. Anyone who looks critically at such statements made by Rahner will see that he does not speak placatively or even polemically, but in a roundabout, relaxed way, though also with extreme acuteness and a sovereign control of the rules of logic. The result is all the more impressive. One need only read again the objective and at the same time inexorable way in which he demolished the arguments of the papal encyclical *Humanae vitae* and the Roman declaration that women cannot be ordained to the priesthood, two recent church documents which he resolutely rejected.[39]

Because for some readers this short book will also serve as an introduction to Karl Rahner, I would also like to add some more personal factors which may have contributed towards making Rahner's articles sometimes seem so complicated. Karl Rahner was an enthusiastic worker. But his background and family upbringing, Jesuit school and a great sense of obligation disciplined him to work incessantly. His life-style was the opposite to the ideology widespread today, that we only realize ourselves when we are doing exclusively what gives us pleasure. Rahner's head was always full of ideas, and when he could develop them freely, for example when he was so absorbed that he thought aloud during a lecture or seminar session, he could produce long texts as it were on the spur of the moment and yet speak quite comprehensibly. But when he had to put anything on the typewriter, he had difficulties(only in the last third of his life was he able to dictate his texts). It did not give him pleasure and yet it had to be. I would like to illustrate the point from letters to me. In a period of three weeks he wrote in four letters: 'I'm sweating over my Chiemsee lecture.' 'I'm now at my Chiemsee lecture but I'm not enjoying it. Already at p.7 (closely written) but that isn't yet a third of it.' 'I can't get on with my Chiemsee lecture. I can't get over the decisive hurdle.' 'The Chiemsee lecture hasn't come out well. When I've finished the Salzburg lecture I will try to improve it a bit. But it probably won't get much better. I don't have the dedication I need.' One can easily see how the torment of production also had its effect on the style of what was produced.

His audience

However, his lectures were a very different matter, especially when he departed from his manuscript. Franz K.Mayr records what we Innsbruck students felt about Rahner's lectures:

> For the students who were familiar, from his introductory courses in Christian philosophy onwards – and their Christian content often seemed to be reduced to the Latin vocabulary – with formidable Latin definitions and distinctions, with theses and their corollaries, two worlds opened up: on the one hand the world of Latin scholasticism and the late scholasticism of the church, usually so dead and therefore so clear and precise, and on the other the living world of Rahner's theology which, precisely because it was alive, was so complex and so directed towards the future. In addition there was something else: the Latin textbooks and also some of the teachers of traditional philosophy and theology who used them were so learned, so mediaeval and so above any further questioning, whereas in Rahner's lectures one can only say that one was caught up into the creative stream of a thinker who was struggling with the substance of theology today and tomorrow in his own mother tongue. The moment when the old bells struck the hour in the old theological faculty building always came too soon when Rahner was in the auditorium... The long sentences, often beginning with a tentative 'Presumably', in the middle dominating a wholeness of thought which was kept under control and at the end asking, ending in a seconds-long silence held the hearer's attention completely; indeed at the end of many lectures one was overwhelmed, not to say exhausted, by the depth of the thought and the richness of what was said. At such times the man, the priest, the member of the Order, the professor – though Rahner did not have an iota of the professor, certainly not of the legendary German professor, about him – were transcended and taken up into Rahner the thinker.[40]

The relationship of his audience to Karl Rahner was therefore not simply that of students to a professor (a beloved professor). Nor was it that of pupils to a master. Rahner himself sometimes said that he had no disciples (in the narrower sense) and in fact no one succeeded in following him in precisely his way of doing theology. Later, now and then he spoke of his pupils,[41] but when he did so he really meant friends. The relationship of 'his' audience to him can best be illustrated by the story of the watch. For his silver jubilee as a priest on 26 July 1957 his closest circle of pupils at that time gave him a watch. I had bought it in Switzerland and had engraved on the back: '26 July 1932-1957 – I Cor.4.15'. In the translation by Otto Karrer in which I had come across it, this verse of the Bible read, 'Though you had countless schoolmasters in Christ, you did not have many fathers.' In a letter of 1 June 1970 he made the quite irrelevant comment: 'Today I have sent to be cleaned the watch which you once gave me (1957). Since that time it has only once been to the watchmaker, and that was more than ten years ago, I think.' And on 16 July 1982 he wrote to me: 'Your watch is still on my wrist and for about twenty years it has never been to the watchmaker. It constantly reminds me of old times which seem to me to have been happier than those of today.' Perhaps the story shows that the relationship is best described in terms of mutual devotion and faithfulness, based on a foundation which has directly to do with God.

Helper in need

Many people turned to Karl Rahner with cares and concerns of all kinds. He helped them as best he could. Most of the questions reached him in the form of letters. He was a zealous correspondent who was a master of the art of expressing himself in the form of letters. Because of the self-discipline that I have already mentioned he had a particular virtue that I have not found in anyone else: he replied immediately, as it were by return of post. He was indefatigably ready to cope with questions from the whole range of pastoral care. Karl Rahner the letter-writer shows this aspect of his help in the book 'My Problem – Karl Rahner Replies to Young People' (*Mein Problem – Karl Rahner antwortet jungen Menschen*, Freiburg 1982). The book includes real letters and Rahner's undoctored replies. These are letters from young people in Vienna on every possible problem of their lives and the answers of a man who was almost eighty.

Another way in which Rahner was 'approached' was through the parlour. He never refused visits and he often acknowledged how much he himself had learned from these contacts and how grateful he was to the visitors, including those with requests. In his time at Innsbruck up to 1964 the pressure of visitors was not controlled by a secretariat or anything like that: anyone who rang the doorbell reached Rahner. He often sighed over the fact that this kept him from other work, but he never let his visitors feel that. I would like to illuminate this activity in the parlour with two quotations from letters of Rahner to me because they discuss the matter directly.

> Although the boy, a chronic addict who cannot be helped, has already talked to me countless times, I asked him back into the parlour and gave him seventy shillings. I think that he has improved in his addiction (to drugs). He also looks a little better. But he has no room, last night he slept on the station, he does not want to go back into the hostel for the homeless, his wife (as he told me earlier) has left him, delivering the shabby *Tiroler Nachrichten* does not bring him in enough money (he will be right there) and recently when doing his round he fell off his bicycle because he was so weak. He does not want to become a seller of the *Flamme* (I would not have much against that, though I did not advise him directly), and so on and so on.
>
> Again all good wishes. I must go back to the parlour. Early today I needed all my human and Christian eloquence to talk someone out of committing suicide. I wonder whether I have succeeded? And what I should have done this morning, the Hamburg lecture, is still not done (11 March 1962).
>
> I'm always caught between two possibilities (I've just given 20 DM again to a man who is perhaps a swindler): either to fall for someone or not to help a really poor devil. What do I do? When I can, I prefer to risk being taken in (2 January 1965).

Rahner was very inventive in detecting sources of help. As a member of an Order he had no money of his own, so he often went to his friends or well-to-do people whom he knew and openly asked them for money. In his first period at Innsbruck he very often helped with serving at table, i.e., with some others in the Jesuit community he served the food from the trolley and then collected up what was left. In this way he diverted some meat and bread to his parlour people.

Of course, the need with which he was confronted was not just of a material kind. Karl Rahner the helper in need here revealed an attitude towards people which was certainly not middle-class. I can give only a few examples here from a wealth of instances which I have continued to remember. A psychology student collected a good deal of material for her diploma work but had such a 'block' that she could not get it down in writing. Rahner wrote the whole work from her material on his typewriter. He helped to make some doctoral students really interested in their dissertations for the first time by formulating key passages himself. In Münster he secured the appointment as an academic assistant of someone who had come into conflict with the middle-class society there and had been in prison. In Innsbruck he defended the existence of the youth hostel directed by P.Sigmund Kripp against the church authorities, who accused the director of allowing 'immoral' relations among the young people. He also took on to the journal a teacher from the Tyrol who had lost her job because in her class she had discussed a drama by F.X.Kroetz including all its 'offensive passages'. In the last two years of his life Karl Rahner often went from Innsbruck to Vienna and stayed in the Caritas Youth Hostel supervised by Fr Georg Sporschill, had confidential conversations with young people, some of whom had serious previous convictions, and readily entered into correspondence with them.[42]

Partner of the media

Finally, I should mention another important area in which Rahner performed as well as he could a service to which he felt committed, the sphere of the media. He approached journalists, camera crews and recording studios with the same openness and confidence as that which he showed to everyone else. He was interested in their life, their work and their equipment. He allowed them to invite him out to eat – preferably ice cream! – and imparted to them the wisdom of ancient ascetics, that God has not created the good things of life only for the villains. But he was no tame society priest, the kind who demonstrates that he can talk fluently and with a smooth tongue in all the salons of the world (although he could make small talk in the company of holders of the Order of Merit, with Federal Presidents, Nobel Prize winners and other distinguished figures of the intellectual world). However, he talked about the incomprehensible mystery that we call God as seriously with journalists as he did with theological students. After his death these journalists showed in obituaries in newspapers, radio and television how much he had affected them at a point on which they did not usually open themselves up.[43]

As a summary of what I have tried to say about Karl Rahner the servant of humanity, I would like to quote some fine comments by the psychotherapist Albert Görres, who for many years was a friend of his:

What kind of a man was that? After the war he begged for food for undernourished families. After a triumphant festive academic gathering for his eightieth birthday he went gently and with some embarrassment back to the desk, this time to ask those present to contribute towards a new motor bicycle for a missionary in Africa - he could not wait for the *adveniat*. At this moment we could understand who this great theologian is: a helper in need for body and soul, one who thinks of a simple or even an amazing solution for extreme distress, of faith, of conscience, of thought and of existence as a whole: a brilliant helper in need who sometimes had as it were to go against God and the world. The man with between three and four thousand publications, including paperbacks with editions amounting to more than a million, would allow himself to be addressed by unknown people on the street and seems to have had inexhaustible resources of time when someone approached him as a pastor. Rahner found helpful thoughts for countless battered heads and wounded hearts, for legions of people who had been (at least in their view) harmed by the church and disappointed by God, thoughts which again opened up an approach to the lost God which had been obstructed, to God's sometimes frightening creation, to his difficult gospel, and not least to his burdensome church, and showed them love. He comforted the sorrowing, taught the ignorant, and showed the right way to the doubters and those who had gone astray. He reconciled those who were not at peace and in all this achieved all that pastoral help can achieve: reconciliation with a reality that seems intolerable, rebellion against all that cannot be accepted. That is also the quintessence of his political theology. Thus Karl Rahner as theologian and pastor is at the same time one of the most healthy 'psychotherapists' for all those people who are alienated, because he is an extraordinary teacher about how to turn towards a healing reality.

Why do so many laity, reluctant believers and well-disposed non-believers, so many natural scientists and doctors, researchers in all disciplines and simple people and children have such a loving respect for the man, although he seems to give them a real intellectual battering? What do they find in him? They find someone who is as deeply trustworthy as experienced doctors used to be in the old days, or country pastors brimful of good will and as pious as they were wise. They find a fellow human being who has learned humanity, a scholar who knows what scholarship is, who can apply his mind, evoke an awareness of problems, pose simple yet difficult questions and answer them with a unique mental grasp. They find someone who listens without being scandalized, full of confidence, who condemns no one, who discovers a positive side in the negative, although he is not sparing with angry words either. They find a theologian who simply wants to understand as well as possible what the faith of Christianity says and what it does not say. And they find a Christian who in the simplicity of his heart speaks and lives from the heart of the gospel.

And at the end of his evaluation of Karl Rahner Görres writes the fine sentence:

Rahner's capacity to speak to the wise and the foolish as partners, over abysses of difficulties in understanding, is connected with his gift of getting into other people's shoes, which according to an Indian proverb is the basis of all understanding.[44]

3 Jesuit

In the year before he died Karl Rahner answered the question why he had become a Jesuit:

Basically I no longer know. If you ask someone who has been married for sixty years why he married Bertha and not Andrea, he may well not be able to tell you. And it's the same with me.

Of course being Catholic, having a feeling for the priesthood, wanting to do God's work – I took such general considerations for granted. But I could also have become a secular priest or an academic interested in religious matters, like Walter Dirks. I am no longer aware of my specific motivations. I think I can remember that I imagined that my specific work within the Order would be something like the pastoral care of students. After philosophy, some of my colleagues on the course were sent to Brazil – that could also have happened to me. At any rate, I do not think that at that time I envisaged being a professor of theology; it was simply that one put oneself at the disposition of the Order and that was that.

In one's younger years one has an enthusiasm which involves the feelings; when one gets old, another atmosphere of experience develops. One can see more clearly than before all the human inadequacy even in an Order and its history. But that does not change the fact that I am glad to have spent my life in such a life-style, doing such work. When I think that I could, for example, have been a lawyer, have had a wife and children, earned a good income, built a house, have had good holidays in Tunisia and played my part in international legal associations, the life of a Jesuit seems to me to have been ten times more enjoyable. Granted, there are other things under the surface of such bourgeois banality – real love for a wife, bringing children into the world and rearing them to be reasonable people. Conversely one discovers dust and ashes, inadequacy and deception in some aspects of an Order. In the last resort all possible ways of living are somewhat laborious and disappointing if one compares them.[45]

He described how he owed his innermost and most authentic relationship to God, his theology and all his other activity, to his Order and especially to its founder Ignatius of Loyola, in the 'Speech of Ignatius of Loyola to a Jesuit of Today' ('Rede des Ignatius von Loyola an einen Jesuiten von heute'), a text which he called his spiritual testament.[46] He thought everything else – specific conditions within the Order, a community in which things were normally done in a sober and matter-of-fact kind of way without much warmth, and the superiors of the time – secondary compared with this. He experienced the depths and the heights in the Order: during the war he learned from the example of his friend and fellow-Jesuit Alfred Delp how the authorities could deal with awkward people.[47] His own personal difficulties began ten years later, brought on by his fellow Jesuits S.Tromp, the dogmatic theologian, and F.Hürth, the moral theologian, both influential advisers to Pius XII. The denunciations in Rome to the effect that he was neglecting Latin in his lectures, which led to the despatch of a *Visitator* to Innsbruck, similarly came from his fellow Jesuits. It became clear to him from the behaviour of the General of the Order, J.B.Janssens (who died in 1965), that while a superior can be respectable and pious he can also lack civil courage or solidarity with those who have been entrusted to him.[48] However, he also experienced heights, beginning with the trust and approval which the next General, Pedro Arrupe, showed towards him, and extending to the warmth with which the new General, Kolvenbach, greeted him.[49] At the end of his long life Rahner, who had often suffered from the atmosphere in the houses of the Order, the briskness with which the old and sick were treated, even experienced something like a wave of human warmth from his colleagues. But all that did not come first for Karl Rahner. The essentials of being a Jesuit remained unaffected by it.

Ignatian

For Rahner, the Order with its Ignatian spirituality was the specific place where outward help from the church met up with the inner grace of God and thus made possible the most important thing in his life, direct experience of God. So in his testament he could say that the main task for Jesuits must be the giving of Exercises: 'help towards direct experience of God in which they realize that the incomprehensible mystery that we call God is near, that it can be addressed and precisely then makes a blessed home within us, if we do not seek to make it subject, but surrender ourselves to it unconditionally. You are continually to examine all your actions to see whether they serve this end. If they do, then biologists among you may also investigate the spiritual life of the cockroaches.'[50]

However, this experience of God at the same time means a recognition of how infinitely important a creature man is, for it is precisely to him that the 'unspeakable God' draws near. Someone who has experienced God not only recognizes God's proclivity towards his creation but also feels summoned to follow this divine proclivity: he can take the finite with real seriousness, recognize it as lovable, beautiful and eternally valid, because God has given himself, and still gives himself, to this finitude. Thus for Karl Rahner being a Jesuit involved the Ignatian invitation to find God in all things. At the same time it represented the deepest foundation of his basic theological principle, that love of God and love of man are one.[51]

This proclivity of God to the world and the individual bears the specific name Jesus, and at the same time in Jesus what it means to be a human being is expressed to the full; therefore in the Ignatian view the incomprehensible God and finite humanity cannot be found through by-passing Jesus. According to Ignatius/ Rahner we have only completely found Jesus, and God in him, when we have died with Jesus, a process which does not take place at the end of a life but is taking place throughout life. This dying with Jesus in God is called following Jesus. Such discipleship takes many forms. Rahner says, with Ignatius: 'I have chosen the discipleship of the poor and humble Jesus, the poor and humble Jesus and no other. Such a choice has the underivability of specific love; it is a call which has its legitimation only in itself.'[52] As Rahner says in the same text, he knew that such a choice would lead to the role of an outsider in both world and church, to the renunciation of power, privileges and honours, and he was convinced that he would best be able to practise this role with the Jesuits. He was then unflinchingly true to it for sixty-two years in the Order.

Churchman

Karl Rahner's radical and not easily understandable attitude to the church grew out of these basic positions involved in his life as a Jesuit. In Rahner there is an innermost nucleus which is connected with his experience of God: 'The church has infinite dimensions because it is the believing community of human beings who are filled with the Spirit of God, making a pilgrimage in hope, and loving God and humanity.' From this description of communal discipleship of Jesus, Rahner – as in other writings –

goes on directly to speak of the institutional, specific church, as if this context can be taken for granted. This is the point at which he would not allow critical questions and at which he refused to be open to objections from biblical criticism and history. With Ignatius he said: 'But I take it for granted that the church is also a socially constituted, specific church in this history, a church of institutions, of the human word, of tangible sacraments, the bishops, the Roman Pope: the hierarchical Roman Catholic church. And if anyone calls me a churchman and I take this for granted, then the reference is to the church in its tangible and harsh institutionalism, the official church, as you tend to say nowadays, with the not particularly friendly overtones that this word has. Yes, I was this man of this church; I wanted to be, and never found here an absolute conflict with the radical immediacy of my conscience to God and my mystical experience.' Rahner criticized the specific church only from this basis of unconditional loyalty and identification, but when he did so it was harshly and without decoration. Therefore this confession is followed by a typical Rahnerian 'but': 'But my membership of the church would be totally misunderstood were it understood as an egoistical, fanatically ideological, limiting power of love which seeks to conquer the conscience; were it understood as identification with a "system" which does not point beyond itself.'[53] Rahner had experienced something that others did not experience in the same way: that the church can point beyond itself into the mystery of God.

Here I should indicate, at least in brief, the degree to which people near to Karl Rahner were convinced that he was truly a man of the church. Rahner did not love the church merely with words, or exploit it – as often happens – as a springboard for a power-obsessed career, as an institution which guarantees an approach to the media and assembled crowds. He often said to me, 'Where would Herr X, with his rabid criticism of the church, be, if the church did not give him a platform?' Johann Baptist Merz rightly says: 'In good Jesuit fashion, Rahner seems almost a natural churchman. So he has this church in his guts, and feels its failures like indigestion.'[54] I have already indicated that Rahner's commitment to the church was perhaps purchased at the cost of a certain loss of critical and argumentative force. In the more than thirty years over which I had a very close and friendly relationship with him, I found him really angry only once. The journal *Publik-Forum* had published a letter from a reader which gave polemical support *for* Kung's criticism of infallibility. Rahner thereupon resolved to leave the advisory body of the journal and said to me: 'Any kind of discussion there is quite impossible for me. And I will not talk with them – that's it, finished.' Metz rightly says in the passage I have quoted that here is one for whom the church has become first nature.

Metz aptly says of a large number of Rahner's theological articles which attempt to defend the teaching of the church and the church itself: 'He was an indefatigable interpreter and sometimes tried to understand and rescue more than could be understood and rescued, to defend more than could be defended.'[55]

Karl Rahner always thought first of the church *as a whole*. In his view the community of true believers is willed and called to life by God. The community of faith *as a whole* has the spirit of God, and is so preserved by God in the right faith that in principle it cannot fall into error. Therefore the church has this 'infallibility' *as a whole*. Only after this again basically anti-élitist view of the church was Rahner concerned with its institutional aspect, with sacraments, ministries and so on. He affirmed it as something that had grown up in history, as a necessary support for the identity and the ordered life of the church as a whole, but he did not overestimate its significance. And it would not have occurred to him to think first of Pope and bishops when he heard the word 'church'.

Karl Rahner's remarks about the papacy show very clearly the kind of false churchmanship with which his own churchmanship should not be confused. They are far removed from any cult of the papacy or enthusiasm for it. Of John XXIII he said: 'Seen from below, and probably also in reality, John XXIII was an almost naive man, basically conservative and old-fashioned to all external appearances. But he had a degree of innocence and the goodwill to come to terms to some degree with the world as it actually is.' Of Paul VI: 'Paul VI, the faithful servant of Pius XII, the cardinal of John XXIII, had to live and die with the situation with which he was confronted. By and large, though perhaps more in letter than in spirit, he accepted the Second Vatican Council, carried it through to the end and respected it.' And then on John-Paul II: 'On the other hand there are people who are frightfully enthusiastic about the Pope but nevertheless do not have the right relationship to him. They are enthusiastic because it is Giovanni again and he also works with a degree of wit; the enthusiasm for the present Pope is precisely the same. Giovanni was all right by me and I can also cope with the present one.'[56]

I have been made to think by the fact that there were no really important conversations between Karl Rahner and church figures in high places, although these people knew of his feelings about the church and he was ready to talk to them. He once said very sadly to me that in the five years that he spent in Münster he was not once addressed by the Bishop there in connection with religious or theological matters. And as he relates, only trivialities were exchanged in the private audiences with Paul VI and John-Paul II.

The following story may indicate the petty anxieties great church figures can have. When Rahner was called to Munich in 1964, he immediately visited Romano Guardini, who was very happy that Rahner should be his successor. Guardini told him of one wish he had for Rahner's future activity in Munich: Rahner should always wear a tie because he, Guardini, had worn one and not a Roman clerical collar. Rahner gladly assented, as he had never regarded a stiff white collar as the mark of the priest nor seen the colour black as the favourite colour of the kingdom of God. When he was received in private audience by John-Paul II in 1979 he wore a tie. The Pope, who had resolved to go back to the old Roman form of dress, did not allow the usual commemorative photograph to be taken at the end. He did not want to be photographed alongside Rahner wearing a tie...

4   The Human Side

Doubtless some things should be reported about a person which are not really shaped by religion or theology, even if the person concerned was a religious person, a theologian. Indeed, those who are interested in him want to know these 'human'features. But what is important here, and what is less important? And now that he is dead, how can a living likeness be captured of Karl Rahner, a bundle of energy grown small?

Mario Galli coined the phrase the 'growling charm' of Karl Rahner. The 'growliness' was also onomatopoeic, stemming from the darkness of his voice which, if he was being terse, was like a snarl. In addition it was connected with Rahner's characteristic dourness, though that did not exclude cheerfulness. He once said of himself: 'For my part, with my Black Forest temperament, i.e. with a degree of sceptical melancholy, I was not someone who from the start led a simple and cheerful life.'[57] He often gave the impression of being miles away, meditating; not least thanks to increasing difficulty in hearing, he could easily withdraw into himself, even when vigorous debates were going on around him. A friend of Rahner's describes how in 1922 he had taken the Bodensee boat to Bregenz on his journey to become a Jesuit novice at Feldkirch in Vorarlberg. On the deck he was struck by a young man who was sitting on an old-fashioned wooden sea chest and gloomily boring into the planks of the deck with a large umbrella – his first encounter with Karl Rahner on the way to the life of the Order.

This serious disposition was combined with an energetic temperament. Right up to his old age Karl Rahner was very restless. Disciplined though he may have made himself at work, he found it difficult to tolerate tedious meetings. His vitality sometimes turned into unfriendliness towards those who interrupted him – though these did not include all kinds of people in need of help.

However, 'charm', too, well describes one side of Karl Rahner's nature. His confident approach to people was charming. He had unbounded curiosity about them, about how they lived, how they fared. He carried on countless conversations and derived from them a considerable knowledge about world affairs, about business concerns, about marital problems; he spoke about scientific questions, with special attention to the sphere of the natural sciences, about literature, and about the graphic arts. On the other hand I cannot recall that he was particularly interested in landscapes. When he spoke with people of all kinds, he was a very attentive listener. He joined in, but never paid compliments; anything false was alien to him. His honesty was part of his charm. However, it was his childlikeness that was most charming. Helmut Erharter and Wilhelm Zauner write in their 'Thank-you to Karl Rahner': 'He loved to go into a toyshop and be shown, to his amazement, what everything was and how it worked: he was a playful person and his brother Hugo has given a marvellous description of this. He could tell clever jokes and laugh heartily at them himself. He enjoyed a good meal with a large glass of beer. He once got off the train laughing, and said, "I've just been in the cinema carriage. The film was called *Wasted Youth*, but there were just three of us watching it, all old men." '[58] When he left Münster in 1972 his students gave him the Kugelspiel Labyrinth. He was occupied for the evening.

He could play with children and was devoted to his relatives. As well as toys, any kind of technology interested him – anything that people can make. He liked being driven very fast in cars and admired anyone who could drive. However, he loved flying more than driving in cars. He had occasion to fly for the first time at the beginning of the 1950s, when he had a lecture trip to Barcelona, and last flew at the beginning of the month in which he died, March 1984, from Budapest to Innsbruck. But he also found great enjoyment circling the peaks of the Tyrolean Alps in a light plane if anyone invited him. It was important for him to be on the move. He was never very keen on real holidays, but he loved moving around to work in different places. In his earlier years he was probably quite proud that he virtually never had a holiday, that he did not engage in any expensive hobbies like photography, and so on.[59] In his old age he became increasingly relaxed, and even took photographs in the last year of his life. When he was studying theology in Holland he had to look after the beehives in the house; he was the 'bee father'. During this period he got used to smoking. When Pius XII suggested to the Jesuits that they should give up smoking for the sake of the kingdom of heaven, he gave up cigarettes for a while - without lasting success. For a while he chain-smoked with the usual consequences of lack of breath and circulation problems. He only gave up this 'hobby' after he was seventy. Brought up from the start to physical reticence and shyness – an attitude which was further emphasized by the Jesuits – at the end of his life the beauty of tenderness dawned on him. Now he could put his arms round people naturally, and even a telephone conversation could end with the words, 'I embrace you'.

Karl Rahner was a faithful and a devoted friend, who as far as possible sought to delight his friends within the bounds of what was possible for a member of an Order with no possessions, and he showed solidarity with them in every conceivable situation. Few are alive from the circle of his fellow students among the Jesuits, from the group with which he started off in Munich before the war and the wartime period in Vienna. The theologians of the 'guild' – above all professors of systematic theology, who were prelates or secular priests – were largely offended because of his criticism of scholastic theology which he expressed early and in sharp terms. Later, when his public success could no longer be overlooked, they greeted him with envy and barely concealed jealousy. So the few from this group who stood by his side were all the more important to him. Two who remained faithful to him into advanced old age deserve special mention: Hermann Volk, Professor of Dogmatics in Münster, and Heinrich Fries, Professor of Fundamental Theology in Tübingen and Munich. He came to know both of these men in connection with ecumenical enterprises and learned to value them. He was invited along with Volk to a symposium on christology held by the French Dominicans at La Tourette near Lyons on 6 and 7 April 1961; that was an occasion for me and Heinz Schuster to make up a foursome to go with him to France. A year later Volk had become Bishop of Mainz. On 7 June 1962 Rahner wrote to me: 'I got home from Mainz very early yesterday. The consecration was very fine, but went on too long. I was next to Grosche. I saw Höfer only in the distance because I had to catch the train straight after the consecration. The previous afternoon (Monday) I had a cup of tea with Volk. Fortunately he was still the same.' Volk, later to become a cardinal, always remained an old and faithful friend of Rahner's, and he wrote him a good letter for his eightieth birthday[60] (both were the same age) and soon afterwards accompanied him to the grave. Heinrich Fries had sought theological conversation with Rahner at an early stage. He insisted that Rahner should participate in the larger ecumenical enterprises and at the beginning of 1983 worked together with Rahner in Innsbruck on a book in which the union of the churches was put forward as a real possibility.

Of the friends of Rahner who are also public figures I must mention here Sylvia and Albert Görres in Munich; Marianne and Walter Dirks in Wittnau; Luise Rinser in Rocca di Papa; and Anita Röper in Mainz. Sometimes they were involved in joint publications with Rahner, sometimes Rahner played a major role in their work, but he always spoke of them with great sympathy and gratitude.

Those who were personally closer to him also included publishers. He did not give his manuscripts to particular publishers primarily because these would provide special promotion and wide distribution, but because he felt ties with one or other of their directors. Of those now dead that was particularly true of H.Dubler of Ars sacra and Heinrich Wild of Kösel. In Benziger Verlag there was Oscar Bettschart; in Herder Verlag Robert Scherer, the same age as Rahner, who as a philosopher performed the service of introducing the thought of M.Blondel to Germany, and was for many years the chief reader in theology, and Franz Johna. Tyrolia in Innsbruck was given *Mission and Grace* because of the reader there at the time, Walter Strolz. Of foreign publishers Paul Brand in Hilversum had particularly good contacts with Rahner.

The collaboration with publishers not only demonstrated human virtues in Rahner like loyalty, commitment and reliability, but also revealed a wealth of riches of a practical kind. He often provided new stimuli for format and sales, and above all he had ideas about how stagnant journals could be relaunched. Once he had made himself known to a journal as an author he soon identified himself with its aims and remained loyal to it even under difficult circumstances. He felt a special tie to the Herderbücherei, with whose leading figures (Johannes Harling, 1902-1979, Ludwig Muth and Leonie Höhren) he discussed the theological programme from 1958 to the day of his death. A few weeks before his death he was able to celebrate his millionth Herder paperback with Herderbücherei.

Karl Rahner was once asked what 'great figures' of his day had seemed to him to be particularly interesting and impressive when he met them. First he mentioned his teacher Martin Heidegger and then continued: 'I knew personally Heinrich Böll, Golo Mann, Erich Fromm and Ernst Bloch; I also met Karl Barth at least once in my life and also Paul Tillich.'[61] However, he then added an illuminating comment about the 'somewhat monotonous self-interpretation of my life': 'I did not really meet particularly great figures who overwhelmed me and radically changed me.'[62] He always wanted to direct attention away from himself, from other people, to the mystery that shapes the life of a human being and finally and ultimately waits for him. Therefore it would not be like Rahner to end this introduction by saying that he was a unique person and that everyone who was closely associated with him felt this to be a great joy, though that is true. Rahner would have replied to such a statement in the same way as he replied to a questioner who asked him about his personal life: 'I do not know what's happened to my life. I did not lead a life; I worked, wrote, taught, tried to do my duty and earn my living, I tried in this ordinary everyday way to serve God – that's it.'[63]

II Life and Works

In the period immediately before the Second Vatican Council Karl Rahner was already a 'concept' to many people in Europe who were interested in religion and theology. However, they had had only a glimpse of him in some of his writings, with their great multiplicity of themes; they were far from having made direct contact with him in lectures, and they often did not really see how the inwardness of his religious language, the sharp logic of his academic discussions and his brusque criticism of the church could be made to hold together. So the question often arose, 'Who is this Rahner?'. A Belgian publishing house, Lannoo in Tielt, took the initiative and asked me, via Piet Fransen, the Jesuit and dogmatic theologian, who was both my friend and a friend of Rahner's, whether I would write an introduction to Karl Rahner's thought and life. Rahner, whom I approached over the matter, was very attached to this publication, as it saw some things very clearly and was able to put right many wrong judgments. He gave me a mass of material for his biography, and in this way the small book appeared in Flemish in 1962, and also in German in 1963; other translations followed. Rahner himself also worked out the outlines of the theological themes which it contains, and dictated them to my then secretary Gerda Rothmund. In this biography Rahner attached particular importance to three things: his friendship in his youth with Pier Giorgio Frassati, the fate of his philosophical doctorate work in Freiburg im Breisgau, and the 'Vienna memorandum' which he wrote during the war. Nothing had previously been written about any of these three things.

In what follows I want to describe Karl Rahner's life in such a way that his 'works' are also brought to the fore. Since these works were sometimes initiatives which lasted over years, in order to avoid mixing themes up and repeating them, it is necessary sometimes to depict the course of an undertaking and then return again to its starting point in Karl Rahner's life. I believe that this approach will demonstrate most clearly the particular character of his works and also their limitations. However, it is impossible here to survey the content of what Rahner says in individual titles of his enormous output. Moreover, I think it best to get to know Rahner from his own writings. This small book is meant to be an introduction, an aid towards understanding him, and after that an encouragement actually to read him.

1   Origins

Karl Rahner was born in Freiburg in Breisgau on 5 March 1904. All his life he had a great devotion to his mother; he visited her as often as he could, but he could not show her his affection. I often went with him to see her and was amazed that he said almost nothing. She must have been the dominant figure of his two parents. In his old age he said of his mother: 'For all her initiatives my mother was a depressively anxious and disturbingly conscientious woman. She experienced life more from the heavy, burdensome side of duty, and perhaps also took on duties which she could have given up. To this degree she kept an eye on my career rather anxiously; afraid, for example, that I might become arrogant. That was her tendency, rather than to become excited or to find my career splendid – that never happened. In her old age she asked whether she had given her children enough love. Of course that's nonsense, because much tenderness and the like is not characteristic of the Alemannian, nor was she capable of it, simply because of the pressure of work. Nor, I think, did we expect it.'[64] Perhaps the following remark of Rahner's in a letter to me of 16 January 1966 is also a good illustration: 'An idea has occurred to me: take a copy of each edition in the different languages (perhaps by now the Italian is also here) and send them to my mother for her ninety-first birthday. She will be "annoyed" and hide them all, but they will delight her.' He meant my little book about him. She combined a humorous and roguish way of talking with her somewhat anxious character. On my last visit, when she was 101 years old, she said to me. 'I think that Karl

should stop now. People notice so much that he is growing old.'
He was with her when she died, soon afterwards.

It is also best for Rahner himself to describe conditions in his
childhood and youth:

I grew up, I must say, in a normal, middle-class, Christian family.
My father was what is today called an assistant principal; then
they were known as 'Baden professors'. For most of his life he
was a professor at the teachers' college in Freiburg. My mother
came from an innkeepers' family. My grandparents had a small
hotel ('Zur Kybburg') on the outskirts of Freiburg. And there
were seven children in my immediate family, as I've already
said. So one could say that I grew up in a middle to lower-
middle class family. There was always something to eat. The
salaries of officials at that time were very modest. For example,
in 1904/05, at the time when I was born, my father had to spend
around one third of his pay just for the rented accommodation
that we first had in Emmendingen near Freiburg. We had no
opportunity for upward mobility. My mother baby-sat to bring
in some extra money. My father had to tutor on the side to
support seven children who eventually attended university-
orientated schools, and all of whom, I believe, got diplomas
and went to study at a university.

Two of my brothers are doctors. One brother was a teacher
at a business school. My oldest sister married a lawyer from
Hamburg. My youngest sister married a mathematician who
worked for a long time at the technical high school in Aachen.
All this was somehow normal, I'd like to think. It was a life-
style common to the middle class fifty, sixty, eighty years ago.
My grandfather was a teacher in a small village (Horben) near
Freiburg. He also served as community clerk in order to earn
enough to feed his three children and to send two of them to
the university. My aunt, my father's sister, was a real farm girl
on a Black Forest farm in the same village.[65]

We shall be talking later about his brother Hugo (1900-1968),
who also became a Jesuit. Karl Rahner once described the milieu
in which he grew up as a 'whole world',[66] despite the material
cares I have just mentioned. The problems that there certainly were
– criticism of society, problems of marriage and sex, educational
matters, were not discussed publicly in the family and in front

of the children. The Catholic middle-class society from which
Rahner came always stood out for its loyalty to the state without
identifying itself by its representatives out of respect. Thus Rahner
saw the First World War, the change from the Kaiser's monarchy
and the Grand Duchy of Baden to a republic, more as the darker
side of life and an indication of how swiftly the glory of the world
passes away, than as an impulse towards his own political activity.
This Christian middle class had an abhorrence of the rising Nazis,
who seemed to it above all to be uniformed thugs and loud-
mouthed proletarians, but that did not prevent them from later
being loyally obedient to the government once it was formed.
Rahner's comments that his father was critical of H.S.Chamber-
lain's *Foundations of the Nineteenth Century* and Spengler's
Decline of the West[67] shows that this group certainly rejected the
Nazi ideology on a purely spiritual and ethical level, but they
really remained blind to its political and ecumenical consequences.
Accordingly, Rahner's interpretation of Nazism seemed faulty,[68]
precisely from a sociological perspective.

2   Religious Beginnings

From 1908 to 1922 Rahner spent his childhood and youth in
Freiburg. Here in 1910-13 he went to the Knabenburg school and
in 1913-1922 to the Realgymnasium (now the Kepler
gymnasium). He was an average pupil who found lessons boring.
From his schooldays he remembered boys and girls being together
in the same class, as were Jews, Protestants and Catholics; the
atmosphere was tolerant, humanitarian and liberal, as things
were in Baden generally. Rahner regularly took part in the Sunday-
school services, as did a number of teachers, who included Josef
Wirth, later to become Chancellor. Rahner thought that he stood
out from his classmates through a certain marked religious sense,
e.g. his own short thanksgiving after mass. At that time he spent
a good deal of time as a sixteen- or seventeen-year-old with the
fourth book of the *Imitation of Christ*, which has the eucharist as
a theme. Along with his older sister and friends he translated
Latin hymns by Thomas Aquinas into German at the Benedictine
monastery of Beuron. Despite these peculiarities, which Rahner

developed out of a quite personal interest, he was tolerated by his fellow pupils and chosen as class representative.[69]

It was important for Rahner that he belonged to the youth movement, which was in search of new life-styles. He belonged to Quickborn ('Fountain of Youth'), a temperance youth movement; 'clergy were involved in it, but did not control it in the narrower sense that it was an official movement under church direction'.[70] In 1920 he took part in the first great conference of Quickborn at Burg Rothenfels on the Main, where he met Romano Guardini for the first time. 'In Easter 1921 a group of us from Freiburg made a trip in which we performed the Dance of Death in the villages, in the evenings, with torches and costumes. Those were times of poverty and we were usually rewarded with eggs. Students and schoolboys, boys and girls were in the same group. I recall that we gave a vigorous performance of the ring dance.'[71]

This is what Rahner says about Pier Giorgio Frassati (1901-1925), who made a deep impression on him:

Around 1920 or 1921, there was an Italian ambassador in Berlin called Frassati. He was a senator and the owner and director of a large Turin newspaper, *La Stampa*. He sent his son, who was a student of mining engineering, to our family to learn German. This young man – he was cheerful and lively and unassuming – lived with us, not a long time, but still enough for a somewhat lasting relationship to develop, especially with my older sister. He was, one could say, a very ardent 'apostle of charity' in Turin. He died in 1925 of polio contracted in the course of this work, and he is honoured in Italy today as a heroic example of a young Christian. It seems that one day he might be beatified in Rome. In a certain way, he was really a remarkable man – athletic, a mountain climber, skier, rider, a cheerful, jolly person who mixed with other students in the liveliest, even wildest way. He told me himself that as a Catholic student in Rome he squabbled with the fascist students from the very beginning. On the other hand, he was an extraordinarily pious person who prayed, who went to Mass almost every day before the rest of the family got up, and who also displayed exraordinary social concern, as we would call it today, for the poor. It seems he died from this work, eventually contracting polio in this environment. And he thought of the poor people until the last hours of his life... He explained to my mother that he would not become a priest because he thought that in the liberal milieu in which he was born he could do more for the church and for Christianity religiously than if he were a priest. On the other hand he was certainly a man that a girl could love.

Rahner was delighted to have known a candidate for beatification, 'with whom I arranged wrestling matches in the forest'.[72] When Frassati's sister brought out his biography in German in 1961, Rahner wrote the introduction to it, in which he recalled his high estimation.

Rahner also said in retrospect: 'Thus in my youth, as in my later days, there were really no occasions for experiencing great radical shifts or changes.'[73] Karl Rahner's teacher of religion, Dr Meinrad Vogelbacher, certainly played a part in his decision to become a priest and theologian. As I, too, had Vogelbacher as a teacher of religion for several years, twenty years later, I can confirm Rahner's judgment that he was a very intelligent, educated, reasonable, if somewhat dry teacher who had studied at the Germanicum in Rome and was formed accordingly.[74] At all events, Vogelbacher will have been able to arouse an interest in a philosophical form of theology in the introspective Karl Rahner. Rahner could not work out exactly in his old age why he wanted in particular to become a Jesuit. The example of his brother Hugo certainly made his decision easier; but they never talked about it, since 'Alemannian Germans do not speak much about such things, even with brothers they especially like'.[75]

For the same reason, Alemannian taciturnity, Karl Rahner's parents heard of his plans not from himself but from his teacher Vogelbacher. Vogelbacher was sceptical: 'No, Karl isn't suited for that. He's too withdrawn and grumpy.'[76] At all events it seemed sensible and significant to Rahner that he should put himself at the disposal of the Jesuit Order. Had anyone asked him what he was suitable for, he would have replied, 'I imagined something like the pastoral care of students as a specific task within the Order.'[77]

On 20 April 1922, three weeks after his school-leaving examination, Karl Rahner entered the novitiate of the Upper German Province of the Society of Jesus. At that time it was in Feldkirch in Vorarlberg, Austria. As we are told by Robert Scherer, who had intimate experience of this time, in the novitiate Rahner devoted himself wholly to questions of the spiritual life, without anything like vocational arrogance and without expressing a particular theological interest. He concentrated on the foundation of the life of the Order and the study of spiritual writers. At the age of twenty he wrote his first article to appear in print, for the journal *Leuchtturm* ('Lighthouse'); it had the significant title 'Why we need to pray' (1924). On 27 April 1924 he gave the scholastic oath to his superiors; this commits the person giving it to the Society of Jesus but not vice versa. Following the custom of the Order, in 1924/25 he spent his first year studying philosophy at Feldkirch; he spent his second and third years of philosophy, between 1925 and 1927, in Pullach, near Munich. Karl Rahner's teachers in philosophy at that time were K.Frank, K.Frick, B.Jansen, J.B.Schuster and A.Willwoll, reputable and solid teachers. Rahner kept a pile of thick small notebooks in which he entered summaries of his studies and extracts from the books he worked through. We can see from them how intensively he was occupied with Kant and the Belgian Jesuit Joseph Maréchal (1878-1944), as also with the French Jesuit Pierre Rousselot (1878-1915). Rahner later mentioned both of these as thinkers who had a great influence on his philosophy; he said that the first real philosophical insight had been given to him by Maréchal.[78] Maréchal had opposed Thomism (which was also taught in Pullach) to the philosophy of Kant and tried to make Kant's transcendental method fruitful for Thomistic epistemology. However, he was also very much concerned with questions of mysticism and mystical experience and in this connection, by asking how 'modern man' was to be understood before God, was a great stimulus to Rahner.[79]

During these first years of his study Karl Rahner's superiors at first intended that he should later teach the history of philosophy at the Philosophical High School of the Order in Pullach. However, before further training it was the custom of the Jesuits to insert a period of practical work between the study of philosophy and that of theology. For Karl Rahner this consisted in having to teach Latin to the novitiate in Feldkirch. At that time Alfred Delp, born in Mannheim in 1907, who became a Jesuit in 1926, was among his pupils. Delp later worked as a sociologist on the journal *Stimmen der Zeit* and thus in 1938 came to belong to a group of

Munich theologians in which Rahner too was active. Delp was among the conspirators of the Kreisau circle against Hitler, was arrested by the Nazis on 28 July 1944 and hanged in Berlin on 2 February 1945. To the end of his life Karl Rahner was proud to have been a friend of Delp's.[80]

3   Theological Studies

Karl Rahner began to study theology in 1929 at the Theological Faculty of the High School of the Order in Valkenburg (Holland). Among his teachers were important scholars of the time, like the exegete A.Bea who later became a cardinal, the exegete and historian of religion K.Prümm, the dogmatic theologians J.Rabeneck and H.Lange, the historian of dogma H.Weisweiler, the moral theologian F.Hürth, the church historian J.Grisar and the ascetic theologian E.Raitz von Frentz. Rahner did not in any way regard the study of theology as secondary because he was destined to teach philosophy. As he himself reported, he put the emphasis on spiritual theology and the history of piety, on patristic mysticsm and also on Bonaventure.[81] He was interested in the mystical idea in the church fathers that the church had sprung from the wound in the side of Christ, a theme on which he later did his doctorate;[82] he investigated the understanding of grace in Clement of Alexandria and Augustine, and studied baptismal theology in the early church. In the very first year of his theological education he read 'almost all the sources of the second Christian century, like the Apostolic Fathers, Justin and Irenaeus, Tertullian and Clement of Alexandria, and also Chrysostom, Gregory of Nyssa and Augustine'; he did intensive study according to a controlled programme.[83]

The situation in theology between the wars

The spiritual situation of the Catholic church in the period before and after the First World War was characterized by a rigidity which we can hardly begin to imagine today. Church thought at this time is usually said to have been shaped by neo-Scholasticism and neo-Thomism. To a large extent that is correct: Rome had attempted to make the philosophy and theology of Thomas Aquinas (died 1274) compulsory – not even in its original form but in its simplified form as transformed by later followers. This kind of prescribed thought included prescribed language: the terms once found in Scholastic theology and philosophy, in Thomas and before him in Aristotle, were to be the only permissible terms, the only correct terms for all cultural circles, to bring the message of Christianity, the content of its faith and its ethical instructions to people of all times. There was a prohibition against questions and experiences which went beyond this stereotyped framework of thought and language. Control was supervised from Rome with the help of a system of clerical informers and willing denouncers spread all over the world who sent reports about all divergences which emerged to the authorities in Rome, the so-called Holy Office, sometimes directly and sometimes through the nuncios. The local bishops, who in any case could only become bishops after following a fixed pattern of ordinariness, adaptability and obedience, had to proceed against rebellious theologians with harsh measures; books had to be withdrawn from bookshops, teachers were not allowed to teach but removed from theological faculties, sometimes banished to monasteries. In Rome there was the 'Index of forbidden books', a list containing all the books and writings which a Catholic was prohibited from reading on pains of spiritual punishment. In 1948 the last official edition of the Index, which was done away with by Paul VI, contained a list of about 4000 titles of books which endangered the faith or were immoral. It might happen that a theologian (like Matthias Laros from Trier) could learn from the newspaper that his books had been put on this Index. Theologians to whose teaching objections had been made were forced explictly to withdraw their teaching and to confess against their convictions. Rome was not content that a theologian should no longer speak on the matter: obedient silence (*silentium obsequiosum*) was prohibited. He had to subject himself, so that it could be said of him, *laudabiliter sese subiecit*, he has laudably subjected himself. Only then had he conformed.

Particularly after the European Enlightenment, Rome attempted to stem the spirit of the time with this and similar means. In addition there were conflicts which were more typical of individual countries. In Germany infection was feared from ideas from the Reformation, open historical research and concentration on the Bible. In France and England Rome fought against so-called Modernism – also influential in other countries – which set individual experience above the dogma of the church and thus attempted to proclaim a Christian faith 'in keeping with the times'. The harsh Roman measures against such burgeoning movements, above all in the time of Pope Pius X (who died in 1914), meant that Catholic theology came to an absolute standstill, especially over exegesis, patrology (study of the church fathers) and church history, and that a climate of hesitation, anxiety and mutual suspicion spread among theologians. The Popes considered themselves the only legitimate and competent possessors and preservers of traditional faith, the *depositum fidei*. They thought that they alone could proclaim the faith 'as right for the times' and in some cases present it in the form of new dogmas. Professional theologians had no independent role here; rather, they had to defend the teachings of the church, above all the dogmas, with the display of their learning.

Even some of Karl Rahner's late remarks are incomprehensible unless one is aware of this situation in which he began to study theology. He often spoke of church 'integralism': by this he meant a view and a way of behaving according to which *all* questions in both the public and the private spheres can only be answered adequately, indeed must be answered adequately, from church tradition, so that in fact there are no independent entities alongside the church. For life within the church the integralist attitude means that all that is traditional must be kept, simply because it is old; that obedience to the authority of the church must be the supreme virtue; and that laity are essentially on the receiving end of commands and have no real initiative.

Rahner also spoke of 'Pian monolithism' because this system, which had entered the church after Pius IX (died 1878) and once again came to a climax under Pius XII (died 1958), threatened to make the church an immovable monolith, a mass of rock, an absolute monarchy, in which everything was governed and decided by the ruler down to the smallest detail. This system was necessarily Eurocentric; i.e., non-European cultures had no chance of introducing their own values into the church: this was a predominantly defensive attitude against the modern world, trapped in a defensive position.

Individuals had constantly protested against such an understanding of the church and the praxis which arose from it. Rome
had often succeeded in silencing them with harsh measures. But
after the First World War movements emerged which were no
longer the concerns of individuals. Common to these movements
was the discovery that in the early Christian period – beginning
from the biblical period – there was a greater richness in ideas,
there were more possible life-styles, than the Roman system
allowed. It was discovered that this heritage could be made
fruitful in the present, and opened up new opportunities for the
proclamation of the gospel in the 'modern' world, while it
nevertheless remained that of the church itself, i.e. did not in any
way rest on a heretical selection. In this way the biblical movement
and the ecumenical movement also arose within the Catholic
church; concern for a renewal of liturgy similarly rested on a
return to the 'sources' as did the concern to renew theology
through intensive study of the church fathers (the theologians of
the first seven centuries).

Gradually a new theology arose through tentative attempts –
and this immediately demonstrated a 'pluralistic' aspect. The
language and methods were different in France at that time from
those in e.g. Germany. The focussing on the Bible, the church
fathers, particular periods of piety and liturgy, involved further
plurality. To understand Karl Rahner one must also understand
that he was already in the second generation of theological
renewal.

The first generation, whose social, spiritual and ecclesial life-
work came to a climax in the period between the two world wars,
introduced the new mentality into theology in a more general way
with a good deal of courage and constant threats from church
officials. This new spirit could not yet have an effect in coping
with the content of particular theological problems. In Germany,
theologians like Peter Lippert, Romano Guardini, Erich Przywara
and others opened up this new period in the sphere of theology.
They represented the new spirit, but hardly went into individual
questions of dogma, so the theological textbooks of the time took
no notice of them. Moreover these theologians above all addressed
people who were active in the new movements, were lively and
interested in religion and spirituality; so they discussed themes in
whch they thought that this circle of readers would be directly

interested. The works of Guardini, Lippert or even Karl Adam are characteristic of this. Finally, in its philosophical and theological youth this generation had experienced the intrigues and heresy hunts within the church and the harsh official reactions, for example against the so-called Modernists, and this had been a trauma. Guardini himself once said that his concern with poets from a theological perspective could be derived from the wish to avoid possible conflicts with the church authorities from the start. In its own way scholastic theology, too, represented such an evasion. If a dogmatic theologian had no desire to converse with contemporary educated people within the church or despisers of religion outside it, he concentrated on editing the texts of old theologians; he worked on a backward-looking history of dogma and left official scholastic theology as it had been before. The textbooks by Bartmann, Diekamp-(Jüssen), Pohle(-Gummersbach), van Noort, Tanquerey and so on in their thorough and respectable way prove that.

From these positions we can understand the character of the second generation. It could no longer be content with the proclamation of a new spirit, an attitude which was quite open to the modern period, its mentality, its art and its problems. Nor could it be content that the new spirit should have an influence only in a renewed church praxis with new pastoral ministries, a new reformed liturgy and so on. It had to devote itself to the whole range of individual questions in philosophy, theology and church life and show the new spirit here, i.e. demonstrate that it was contemporary and also of the church, not just generally but in the vast range of individual problems.

At the beginning of his work as a theologian Karl Rahner was convinced that only if this were really achieved could Christians feel the present to be a natural sphere of existence and completely appropriate to Christianity (as far as that is possible in a world which is in the grip of evil); only then does it emerge that a theologian can do more than defend Christianity against a new period, namely show Christianity to be the new answer of God, only really completely understandable today, to the questions which are raised by our historical present and the future which is emerging. Karl Rahner saw this himself and acted accordingly. With courage and energy he fought alongside the first generation against the system of neo-scholasticism and the Pian monolith for the rights of a new pluralistic theology,[84] and he tried to play his part in fulfilling the tasks of the second generation. This concern was there right from the beginning of his studies.

However, something more must be said of Rahner's precise position in the light of his basic studies. Among the Jesuits the renewal movement in the first half of this century was moulded by a new theological interest in Ignatius and the Exercises. As K.H.Neufeld has shown, the brothers Karl and Hugo Rahner collaborated, at a time when Karl was still studying theology, to to give the spiritual foundation of the Jesuits a deeper basis,[85] the theology of prayer in the Exercises. It was out of this concern that Karl Rahner's first major publications emerged in 1932 and 1933: about the doctrine of the spiritual senses in Origen and Bonaventure amd the spiritual teaching of Evagrius Ponticus. Neufeld pointed out that Rahner's thoughts in *Spirit in the World*, which came soon afterwards, are not the consequences of a break in which for Rahner philosophy forced theology into the background, but that they are rooted rather in concern with the practice of prayer among the Jesuits, just as conversely the significance of the senses for knowledge in Thomas Aquinas is part of the idea that the human senses have their irreplaceable value in converse with God. Thus the old Rahner could say: 'The spirituality of Ignatius himself which we shared in through the practice of prayer and a religious formation has become more significant for me than all learned philosophy and theology inside and outside the Order.'[86]

The group of themes in the first week of the Exercises prompted the two Rahner brothers to turn their attention to repentance and penance. While Hugo concentrated more strongly than Karl on baptism, as a theological student Karl made a thorough study of the history of Christian penance through the standard literature of the time, books by K.Adam, P.Boschmann, P.Galtier, K.Holl and so on. These themes then offered as it were the first test area where the neo-scholastic constrictions could be broken through on the basis of the broader and more elastic views that had been possible earlier.

On 26 July 1932 Karl Rahner was ordained priest by Cardinal Michael Faulhaber in St Michael's Church, Munich, along with sixteen other Jesuits, eight Franciscans and three Benedictines. His study of theology lasted until 1933, and was followed, in accordance with the Constitutions of the Order, by the silent year of the Tertiate, which Rahner spent in St Andrea in the Lavanttal in Carinthia.

4   Philosophy Again

In 1934 Rahner's superiors in the Order sent him to his home town of Freiburg to qualify in philosophy there, since he was 'destined' to become a professor of the history of philosophy. At that time the philosophical faculty at Freiburg was a very interesting and stimulating place for anyone with such an aptitude. Along with Heidelberg, Freiburg had had the good fortune that since 1890 'real' philosophers and not historians of philosophy had been active in the so-called Baden school of neo-Kantianism. In 1928 Martin Heidegger came to Freiburg. He had started from neo-Kantianism, but since 1927 had made his own radical way. When Rahner and his fellow-student Johannes B.Lotz, who had been ordained with him, arrived in Freiburg, the time of the rectorate of Heidegger, who had declared himself an unqualified supporter of Nazism, had just come to an end. The two young Jesuits did not know whether or not Heidegger would accept them as doctoral students; he would have done, and shortly beforehand, turning away from Nazism, he had protected Jews and practising Catholics in his seminar. As a precaution, the two reported as doctoral candidates to Martin Honecker (1888-1941), the Catholic occupant of the Concordat chair of Philosophy. According to the rules the doctorate had to involve two further specialisms, so two other well-known Freiburg scholars became Rahner's teachers – Erik Wolf the philosopher of law and Johannes Spörl the historian. It was not easy to get to Heidegger's seminars, and the demands were even harder; thorough and independent minutes had to be made of the seminar sessions and read aloud in the next session, 'and if you then heard Martin Heidegger solemnly say, "The minutes are excellent", you felt as if you had won a medal'.[87] Rahner kept these minutes, Heidegger's interpretations of Plato, Aristotle, Kant and the pre-Socratics. All his life Karl Rahner revered Heidegger as a great philosopher, though he thought less of Heidegger's thought and the 'shift' in this thought. Heidegger was significant for Rahner because, 'He taught us how to read texts in a new way, to ask what is behind the text, to see connections between a philosopher's individual texts and his statements that wouldn't immediately strike the ordinary person, and so on. In this way he developed an important philosophy of Being. That can and will always have a fascinating significance for a Catholic theologian, for whom God is and remains the inexpressible Mystery.' 'In my manner of thinking, in the courage to question anew so much in the tradition considered self-evident, in the struggle to incorporate modern philosophy into today's Christian theology, here I have certainly learned something from Heidegger and will, therefore, always be thankful to him.'[88] In this sense, but also with these limitations, one can call Karl Rahner a Heidegger pupil. He was certainly less so than other members of the so-called Catholic Heidegger school like J.B.Lotz, G.Siewerth, B.Welte and M.Müller. The estimation was nevertheless mutual. At the end of the 1950s Heidegger, who did not travel much, paid Rahner a visit in Innsbruck, and in a letter of 24 February 1973 Heidegger wrote to me, among other things, 'I have the most splendid memories of working with Fr Rahner during the years 1934-36 in the seminars.'

However, Karl Rahner had to agree on a dissertation with Honecker. It was to be on Thomistic epistemological metaphysics; here 'Thomistic' did not mean so-called Thomism, i.e. the views of the commentators on and followers of Aquinas, but those of Thomas Aquinas himself, which since Gottlieb Söhngen have been called 'Thomanic'. Rahner wanted to write a philosophical and not a historical work. Hence his choice of theme, because the metaphysics of finite knowledge is the first stimulus to philosophizing for Thomas, though – since Thomas means to be a theologian – it is never developed systematically at any length in his writings. Karl Rahner demonstrated that this approach at the same time contains within itself the whole of Thomas' teaching on human knowledge and comes together to form an original unity: human knowledge comes about first and foremost in the world of experience, as the human spirit is always directed towards the phenomenon (*conversio ad phantasma*). Rahner developed this systematically in his interpretation of Thomas, starting from the nature of the human question that a person puts when he already finds himself in the world and asks about being as a whole. The consequences of this approach extend a long way. The knowing being in a thing in the here and now is called 'sense', and knowledge of being as a whole is called 'intellect'; thus there must be an original unity between them. So Thomas also says that neither sense nor intellect as such can be specifically encountered in themselves; the one is different from the other only in its unity with the other. Therefore the problem of the metaphysics of knowledge does not lie in the question how the gulf between knowledge and object is bridged – this 'gulf' does not appear in Thomas himself but is a rationalistic pseudo-problem raised by the interpreters of Thomas; it lies more in how the known, which is identical with the knower, can stand over against the knower and how there can be a knowledge of another as such. From here Rahner develops this possibility in terms of the origin of the senses from the spirit – and not vice versa! This basic insight also remained fundamental for the later Rahner. The primary element in man is the spirit, because it is knowing and awareness, but it is not separate from matter, not something alien and different from it. For Rahner a purely materialistic standpoint is therefore unacceptable, even in dialogue, because the spirit is always already in itself, since it emerged from matter, whereas matter does not know of itself what it is. In an introduction to Rahner's life and work this theme does not need to be developed further. It is enough to cite the closing sentences of the study, which show where Rahner the theologian had got to at the end of this philosophical investigation:

> The theologian Thomas is concerned with man as the place in which God shows himself in such a way that he can be heard in his word of revelation, *ex parte animae*. In order to be able to hear whether God is speaking we must know that he is; so that his word does not come to one who already knows, he must be hidden from us; for him to speak to human beings his word must reach us where we already are, in our earthly place, in our earthly time. In that man is in the world *convertendo se ad phantasma*, the disclosure of being generally and in it the knowledge of the existence of God has always already taken place, but at the same time this God is always already hidden from us as being beyond the world. *Abstractio* is the disclosure of being which places man before God, *conversio* is entering

into the here and now of this finite world which God makes the distant unknown. *Abstractio* and *conversio* are the same thing for Thomas: man. If man is understood in this way he can hear whether God does not say something because he knows that God is; God can speak because he is the unknown. And if Christianity is not the idea of an eternal ever-present spirit but Jesus of Nazareth, then Thomas's metaphysics of knowledge is Christian if it calls a man back into the here and now of his finite world, as the eternal also entered into it, so that man finds it and himself again in it.[89]

Here Rahner was in the midst of a reflection on the foundations of theology. In modern conditions, this could no longer say in the classical terms of fundamental theology: 'If God speaks, man has to obey; now we prove that God has spoken, naturally and supernaturally, so all who do not hear are either intellectually inept or morally perverse.' Modern thought raises the question: Why can a human being hear God at all? How does such a reception of a revelation of God take place, and in such a way that the hearer can stand surety for it, can share it with us in a credible way? This is where Rahner's theological programme began, in the steps of Thomas, in conversation with Kant, German Idealism, Heidegger, but also guided by Ignatius and the significance which human senses have for him in relationship with God. This course led to the elements of a Christian anthropology, a theological doctrine of man. And precisely by reflecting on *conversio*, the necessary self-surrender of man in the world, Rahner found further important additional elements for his theology: what has 'always' been given only becomes concrete and capable of being experienced by us when we begin from ourselves and address ourselves to the individual.

However, Martin Honecker, who was in charge of Rahner's doctorate, was not interested in this epistemological result and the wider horizons that it opened. He criticized Karl Rahner for being misled by his starting point in Thomas to succumb to the dynamics of the subject. Of course that was, and is, a basic problem. How is a philosopher from an earlier period really to be understood properly today? Rahner clearly had views about *his* method of exposition: 'If in this sense the reader gets the impression that here an interpretation of Thomas is at work which derives from modern philosophy, the author regards such an observation not as a deficiency but as an advantage in the book, precisely because he did not know on what basis he could deal with Thomas other than the questions which concern *his* philosophy and the philosophy of his time.'[90]

That was the method of interpretation which Rahner had learned from Heidegger, and when Honecker rejected Rahner's doctoral work this may have been through antipathy to Heidegger or envy of Heidegger's famous seminar. At all events, as Rahner himself reports: 'My dissertation director, Martin Honecker, failed me. Lotz finished his doctoral work under Honecker at the last minute. I was the next one to hand in a dissertation. But I was failed by the Catholic Honecker for being too inspired by Heidegger.'[91]

Though Rahner could not be given the title Doctor of Philosophy – the Philosophical Faculty of the University of Innsbruck gave him an honorary doctorate in 1970 – he prepared the rejected work for publication. It appeared in 1939 from the publisher Felizian Rauch in Innsbruck; it was 296 pages long and entitled *Geist in Welt* ('Spirit in the World'). According to Rahner, Geist, spirit, denotes the human force which reaches beyond the world and recognizes the 'metaphysical'. 'World' denotes the reality which is accessible to the immediate experience of human beings. The title of the book indicates the unity of the two. As might be expected, the book was praised by some for the intellectual capacity of its author and criticized by others for its way of interpreting Thomas. At Rahner's request Johann Baptist Metz prepared a second edition in which the critiicsms were included. It appeared from Kösel Verlag, Munich, in 1957 and was 414 pages long.

5 'Undestined'

In 1936 Karl Rahner returned from Freiburg to Innsbruck. His superiors had planned for, or 'destined', as they put it, him to teach theology in Innsbruck. On the basis of his earlier patristic studies, in a short time he produced a doctoral work in theology which satisfied the requirements of the time: *E latere Christi. Der*

Ursprung der Kirche ab zweiter Eva aus der Seite Christi des zweiten Adam. Eine Untersuchung über den typologischen Sinn von Jo 19,34 ('*E latere Christi.* The Origin of the Church as Second Eve from the Side of Christ the Second Adam. An Investigation of the Typological Significance of John 19.34'). This work, so far unpublished, is iv + 136 pages long. On 19 December 1936 he received his doctorate in Innsbruck. Immediately after that he had to qualify for teaching. According to the laws which used to apply throughout Austria that was not difficult if one had already published academic studies. So the five articles on the spiritual theology of Origen, Evagrius Ponticus and Bonaventure, which had been published between 1932 and 1934, were enough. The theological faculty of the University of Innsbruck granted him his doctorate on 1 July 1937. From the winter semester of 1937 he began to teach dogmatics there. Between these two dates Karl Rahner gave fifteen lectures in the summer of 1937 at the Seventh Salzburg High School Week 'On the Basis of a Philosophy of Religion'. These later gave rise to the book *Hörer des Wortes* ('Hearers of the Word'), which was published during the war, in 1941, by Kösel Verlag Munich; it was 229 pages long. In it Rahner was concerned not only to provide an epistemological foundation for the philosophy of religion as a theological discipline but also to deal with the basic question of the relationship of man to God, whether and how man is positively open to a revelation of God, though this revelation need not necessarily happen. So the question is metaphysical, and not yet positively theological, but it arises out of that common ground between the philosophy of religion and theology where there is reflection on the nature of human beings. Man is spirit, but spirit in the world, in space and time. So he can only be spirit if he turns to the phenomenon, to as many phenomena as possible. For the richer and more varied these phenomena are, the more there appears in them the goal of the human spirit, 'Being itself, which also extends beyond the world.'[92] At the same time, however, man himself is a phenomenon: the most spiritual one. So in him, Being too can manifest itself most fully. And it does so where humanity develops itself most fully. Here Rahner mentions before all else the history of humanity. If the absolute infinite Being did not speak, it would still be there, and in that case the most essential thing in human history would be God's silence in it. But the history of humanity remains the place at which God speaks, and in his innermost nature man is the one who listens to the word of God or waits for God to communicate himself. 'Only the one who thus listens is what he really has to be, man.'[93] So Karl Rahner attempts a definition of man: 'Man is the being of receptive spirituality who stands in freedom before the free God of a possible revelation, which, if it comes, takes place in his history in the world.'[94] For Rahner, human thought can reach that far. To perceive the word and expound it is no longer a matter for the philosophy of religion but the task of theology. At the author's request Johann Baptist Metz also produced a new edition of this second book by Karl Rahner. He expanded the content with later important arguments for the theme like a more exact concept of revelation and the concept of an experience of transcendence. This new edition appeared from Kösel Verlag, Munich, in 1963, 221pp. long; an English translation was published by Seabury Press, New York, in 1969.

6　Brother Hugo and the Beginning of Theological Teaching

This is not the place to evaluate the character and life-work of Hugo Rahner.[95] But as the years before the Second World War were a time when the two brothers were doing theological work together, I must summarize here the basic information about Hugo Rahner's life. He was born in Pfullendorf on 3 May 1900, grew up in Freiburg, became a Jesuit, studied philosophy in Valkenburg and Innsbruck between 1920 and 1923, worked as a teacher in Feldkirch between 1923 and 1926, did his theological study at Innsbruck between 1926 and 1930, was ordained priest in 1929, qualified in theology in 1931, studied history in Bonn between 1931 and 1934 with F.J.Dölger and W.Levison, qualified in philosophy in 1934, was recognized as lecturer in early church history and early Christian literature at the Theological Faculty of the University of Innsbruck in 1937, spent the years between 1938 and 1945 in exile in Switzerland, where he worked with the Eranos conferences, and became Dean of the Theological Faculty of Innsbruck in 1945. He was Rector of the University in 1949/

50, and Rector of the Canisianum, the international theological study centre, from 1950 to 1956. He had to give up lecturing at the end of 1962 because of a serious illness; between 1964 and 1968 he worked in the Jesuit writers' house in Munich, and died on 21 December 1968.

From 1932 onwards the first academic publications by his brother Karl had appeared in French in France; the renewal movement in theology there was deeply concerned with the church fathers, and therefore the journal *Revue d'Ascétique et de Mystique* was interested in the works. Hugo Rahner had made important contacts in Louvain, Brussels and Paris in connection with his Bonn dissertation about a seventeenth-century French figure. These contacts were very helpful for his brother Karl even before the war, and still more afterwards. In 1936 Karl Rahner planned to produce a German version of a book by the French Jesuit M.Viller, 'History of the Spiritual Life in the First Centuries of the Church'. He asked the author's permission to expand the text and change some details; Viller gladly and generously consented.[96] When the book appeared under the names of Viller and Rahner from Herder Verlag in the spring of 1939 under the title *Aszese und Mystik in der Väterzeit* ('Asceticism and Mysticism in the Patristic Period'), its original extent had doubled to almost 340 pages. This work was the result of an intensive collaboration between Hugo and Karl Rahner. It shows the interest of both in history which is not backward-looking but, as Karl Rahner said in the Preface, seeks to gain 'breadth and openness from the past for the future'. Neufeld rightly said of the book: 'This book is particularly significant for the dogmatic work of Karl Rahner since here asceticism and mysticism, spirituality and piety are in no way thought of as a special area, subsidiary to academic theology, but denote the wealth of lived Christian faith, the riches of which have a spiritual effect in human history.'[97] The direct collaboration of the two brothers came to an end with this book.

When Hugo Rahner, along with other Jesuits from Innsbruck, called for a special theology of proclamation which was to be formulated alongside academic theology for the purposes of church praxis (Hugo Rahner produced his book *A Theology of Proclamation*, English translation Herder 1968, to this end), Karl Rahner did not join in. He saw the danger that a merely kerygmatic theology could very easily set aside justified rational, intellectual claims and thus lose its power to convince critics and doubters. So he said, even against his own brother: 'But in fact the strictest theology, that most passionately devoted to reality alone and ever on the alert for new questions, the most scientific theology, is itself in the long run the most kerygmatic.'[98]

In the *Lexikon für Theologie und Kirche* (= *LTK*; 'Lexicon for Theology and the Church'), Hugo Rahner was an extremely helpful, knowledgeable specialist in patrology and thus once again collaborated with his brother. In addition to their work together, however, Neufeld also mentions a parallel set of themes which united the two brothers in the years before the war, in connection with three questions with which Karl Rahner was later intensively concerned. In 1936 both worked on christology, Karl on 'contemporary Protestant christology' – in which he already indicates that he sees in Jesus the basic model of the God-man relationship – and Hugo on the christology of the early church in the light of present-day questions. Karl Rahner began his teaching activity in Innsbruck with the dogmatic 'tractate' on the doctrine of grace. For this he worked out a text, *De gratia Christi*, in which he took the book of his teacher Hermann Lange (*De gratia*, Freiburg 1929) as a basis, but divided the material differently, and considered new problems and new publications. In the late 1930s, in addition to his study of Augustine and Semi-Pelagianism he also wrote an article 'On the Scholastic Conceptuality of Uncreated Grace', which already indicated his view of grace as God's communication of himself. In parallel to that, Hugo Rahner gave lectures on the history of the doctrine of sanctifying grace. And finally, over this period both were engaged in the Ignatian mysticism of delight in the world, which is not a shallow enthusiasm for the world but is integrated into the discipleship of the cross, as Hugo stressed on the basis of the mysticism of Ignatius.[99]

In this way Karl Rahner's style of working had already been outlined. At least to begin with he did not plan complete books, which he would then have had to work out thoroughly, but turned his attention to individual questions which he worked on in the form of journal articles. In addition to the French journal which I have already mentioned, he wrote above all in other Jesuit journals, namely in the German *Zeitschrift für Aszese und Mystik* (since 1947 *Geist und Leben*), the Innsbruck *Zeitschrift für*

Katholische Theologie, the Swiss *Orientierung* and in *Stimmen der Zeit*. From 1935 to 1956 he regularly wrote reviews of theological books for the *Zeitschrift für Katholische Theologie*, which unlike many reviews today show him to have been a thorough and critical reader and indicate what he was reading. From H.Bouillard, H.Rondet, H. de Lubac, Y.Congar via E.Schillebeeckx to C.Boyer and J.Maritain, hardly a name of the significant theologians of the time is missing.

Despite his independent, almost stand-offish manner, Karl Rahner had a marked inclination towards team work. The more clearly he recognized the questions of faith and the theological problems to be coped with, the more clearly he became aware that not one of the tasks could be tackled alone. In later years he not only involved himself in communal enterprises (like dogmatics conferences and the promotion of journals and handbooks) but was also ready for a good deal of other shared work. In 1938 he belonged to a group of theologians who met in Munich and planned joint projects. They included A.Delp, P.Bolkovac, H.U.von Balthasar, A.Lieske (at that time all Jesuits) and Dr Robert Scherer from Herder Verlag in Freiburg. Above all with Hans Urs von Balthasar he produced a new outline of dogmatics which was later published in the first volume of his *Schriften*. The idea of a series of works entitled Quaestiones Disputatae was also born at that time; this was to take up again a tradition from a good period of Catholic theology: discussion instead of declamation, questioning instead of ready listening to prepared answers, acknowledgment of the incomplete and the unready.

First of all political events prevented the further implementation of this theological activity.

7 'District Prohibition'

In March 1938 the Nazi Germans marched into Austria. They quickly exploited the initial enthusiasm of the Austrians and the cultural inferiority of the Austrian Catholics and allowed themselves far more intervention in the church than in Germany at that time. On 20 July 1938 they abolished the Theological Faculty of Innsbruck. The professors moved their teaching into the buildings of the Jesuit college in the Sillgasse where the normal life of the Order and daily work could continue. On 15 August 1939 Karl Rahner made his final vows to the Order, his profession, in the Novitiate of the Austrian Jesuits in St Andrea in the Lavanttal.

In October 1939 the Jesuit College in Innsbruck was also dissolved by the Nazis. Karl Rahner was banished from the Tyrol; he was under a 'district prohibition'. The Prelate of Vienna, Karl Rudolf, a confidant of the then Cardinal of Vienna, Cardinal Innitzer, offered him refuge in Vienna and there took him on to the diocesan administrative staff – Rahner was given the title Ordinariatsrat – and into the Pastoral Institute. Rudolf has given an account of the work of this Vienna group against the Nazis and their fearless involvement in theology and pastoral care in his book *Aufbau im Widerstand. Ein Seelsorgebericht aus Österreich 1938-1945*, which was published by Otto Müller Verlag in Salzburg in 1947; it also describes Karl Rahner's contribution during those years. Rahner gave lectures, especially in the Pastoral Office and the Minorites church, on the Christian picture of man, anthropology as the starting point for theology, and the philosophy of Heidegger (the Parisian journal *Recherches de science religieuse* also published Rahner's article 'Introduction au concept de Philosophie existentiale chez Heidegger' in 1940). He also gave complete courses on dogmatics, and spoke on questions of asceticism and mysticism, sexual ethics and problems of lay people in the church. Despite the dangers of the situation, in this period between 1939 and 1944 Rahner travelled from Vienna to Leipzig, Dresden, Strasbourg and Cologne to give lectures. In this way Rahner the travelling lecturer was 'born', and at the same time these lectures provided constant new material for theological articles.

I would like to mention at least briefly a particular event in those years in Vienna. On 18 January 1943 the then Archbishop of Freiburg, Conrad Gröber, wrote a twenty-one page letter to the 'Most Honourable Episcopate of Greater Germany'. In this letter the Archbishop made vigorous complaints about innovations 'in the sphere of the Catholic doctrine of faith and liturgy', which he summed up in seventeen points.[100] He ended his letter with the words, 'Can we Greater German bishops and can Rome still keep silent?' The letters was regarded by some bishops as over-hasty and uncollegial. The Viennese Cardinal entrusted his Pastoral Office with the production of a thorough counter-memorandum which was written by Karl Rahner (fifty-three pages and a two-page list of contents). This 'Vienna Memorandum' still has not been published,[101] but important ideas from it found their way into the first article in the first volume of Rahner's *Schriften*. It was a programmatical document. Thirty-four pages were devoted to theology. Rahner considered basic problems: what is the significance of the revolution of the time, the dawn of a new age, at any rate for theology? How can the younger generation be addressed? And how is the tradition of the church preserved despite the new language? He pointed out the importance of discussions and controversies, and how fatal embittered silence was. He gave a thorough account of the then state of German theology, made comparisons with France, and considered the relationship between exegesis and dogmatics. He went into the objections of the Freiburg Memorandum in detail and ended by saying that there was no occasion for prohibitions and warnings from the church office, but there were many reasons for a positive encouragement of theological work. He made practical suggestions for this. Nineteen pages of the Vienna memorandum are devoted to philosophy. Rahner stressed the classic figures of modern philosophy, the liveliness of their thought, the duties of Christians and theologians to make contact with such thinkers – all of whose works, *Opera Omnia*, like those of Kant and Nietzsche, had often been put on the Index of books forbidden to Catholics – to allow themselves to be asked questions and learn from them, and also 'to translate the language of one philosophy into that of another'.

The memorandum is interesting for our knowledge of what kind of man and theologian Karl Rahner was: a theologian with acute thought who analysed clearly, who had numerous ideas and proposals for praxis, who did not tactically skate round individual problems but had the great 'strategy' of the church in mind, who was troubled by the questions: How do I translate the old message for today? How can I see that it 'communicates'? The Vienna memorandum was sent to the 'Greater German' bishops and to some relevant institutions. I do not know whether it was read and taken to heart.

8   A New Beginning

In summer 1944 public work in Vienna was a thing of the past.
For the holidays Rahner had taken a post as a locum tenens in the
small village of Mariakirchen in Lower Bavaria and could not
return to Vienna because of the advancing front. He remained in
this village from July 1944 to August 1945 and took over pastoral
care for the inhabitants and the refugees. In August 1945 he was
called to the Berchmans College in Pullach, near Munich, where
the Jesuits were again opening up their theological studies. There
he had to teach dogmatics: in addition he took on considerable
work in bombed-out Munich, giving advice and help to those in
need and delivering lectures and sermons (I have already spoken
briefly of his sermons in Lent 1946 on the 'Need and Blessing of
Prayer'). In the Munich educational centre between 1945 and
1948 he gave courses for those interested in theology: in them he
went through the whole gamut of Catholic dogmatics five times.

In August 1948 he was called back to the re-established
Innsbruck Theological Faculty. He took over from his predecessor
F.Mitzka the dogmatic tractates that Mitzka had been assigned:
in a three-year cycle he had to give lectures on the doctrines of
creation and original sin, on the doctrines of grace, justification,
faith, hope and love, and on the doctrines of the sacraments of
penance, anointing the sick and ordination. As I have already
said, he had to give these lectures in Latin, though the really
interesting explanations and excursuses were given in German.
In addition he had to give an *Exercitatio scholastica*, an exercise
for students in which they were initiated into the art of attacking
and defending theses from the lecture material in Latin, taking on
different roles; this art was customary from the Scholasticism of
the twelfth and thirteenth centuries onwards, but nowadays is
forgotten. His audience in Innsbruck had an international stamp.
The Jesuits maintained the Canisianum as a theological centre in
which, in the wake of a century-long tradition, students from
Germany, Switzerland, the USA, England and Spain lived. In
addition there were students from the priests' seminary of the
bishopric of Innsbruck and some members of Orders, of course

also including Jesuit students. Almost all were training for the priesthood. In the time when I was with Rahner in Innsbruck, between 1950 and 1958, there was only one woman in the audience, Herlinde Pissarek-Hudelist, who is now Professor for Catechetics in the Innsbruck Faculty, occupying the chair which was at that time held by J.A.Jungmann.

Karl Rahner was nominated *ordinarius* Professor of Dogmatics at the Theological Faculty of the University of Innsbruck on 30 June 1949. With the normalization of conditions in Central Europe he also resumed his lecture tours. From the end of the 1940s they took him increasingly further afield, to Belgium, Holland, Spain and Switzerland, and after 1948 he gave numerous radio lectures. So Innsbruck, too, became a new attraction: it was not only the Papal Theological Faculty, a place for the solid education of Jesuits, the home of the 'theology of proclamation', famous through scholars like Hugo Rahner and Josef Andreas Jungmann, but there was also – Karl Rahner. Students gathered in Innsbruck who had come there especially because of him. So now he had to hold seminars which were specially tailored to his pupils and their interest in his theology, and at the beginning of the 1950s his first group of doctoral students came into being: it consisted of Adolf Darlap, Walter Kern, Johann Baptist Metz and me. As Rahner had no assistants and no academic helpers during his time as professor in Innsbruck (1949-1964) – from 1958 to 1962, Franz K.Mayr helped him as a kind of private secretary, and then Frau Pissarek-Hudelist from 1960 to 1964 – these pupils readily served as assistants in various ways. This involved above all the expansion of the lecture manuscripts, which were duplicated for the use of his audience. There were three 'codices' in Latin: the first, on grace, had already been written before the war and in its fourth edition of 1954 had exactly 350 pages; the second, on creation and original sin, was written in 1950, and its second edition of 1953 had 298 pages; the third, on the history and theology of the sacrament of penance, had already been written in Pullach in 1946, its fourth edition of 1960 extending to 785 pages. Various articles by Rahner came into being from the group of themes covered by these writings: on grace; on faith, hope and love; on justification, also in ecumenical terms; on the relationship between the Christian view of creation and evolutionary thought in the natural sciences, on the burden of damnation for humanity and 'monogenism', the doubtful view that humanity descended from just one human couple. In the years between 1949 and 1955 Rahner also wrote articles on the history of theology, relating to the penitential doctrines and praxis of the early church; these were collected together and republished in Vol.XI of his *Schriften*.

9 Creative Initiatives

Karl Rahner's life in which with an almost inconceivable intensity of work and movement around Europe he began projects, seized initiatives and transformed his modest study and bedroom in Sillgasse, Innsbruck into a unique production line.

He was not selective over accepting invitations to lectures, for example judging the likely size of his audience or its level. He spoke to directors of Exercises, superiors of Orders and abbots, doctors and psychiatrists, youth chaplains, journalists and sociologists, teachers and academics of all kinds, social workers, associations for wives and mothers, pastoral congresses, family and educational groups, philosophical societies, to the German liturgical commission and the study group of the Belgian *Lumen Vitae*. He gave visiting lectures at universities in West Germany, Switzerland, Holland and also in Rome.

I would like to stress his involvement in three important circles of discussion. For the first time in 1948 he spoke in Bad Driburg at a conference of Protestant and Catholic professors of theology who were concerned about ecumenical union. From then on, for a long time he was an active member of their council, which was called the 'Jaeger-Stählin group' after its protectors, Stählin the Protestant district bishop and Jaeger the Archbishop of Paderborn. The group also included theologians who became members of the Vatican Secretariat for the Promotion of the Unity of Christians when it was formed in 1960. I have already mentioned Hermann Volk, who later became a cardinal. Prelate Josef Höfer, First Secretary at the Federal German Embassy to the Holy See, was very important for Karl Rahner because of his friendly relations with Roman circles, for example with Fr Augustine Bea SJ, who later became a cardinal.

In 1957 the Catholic Görresgesellschaft for the Advancement of Science set up an international institute for the encounter of science and faith. Karl Rahner belonged to it; he took an active part in the annual conferences (often in Feldafing in Bavaria), and there presented his view on questions of hominization, genetic engineering and so on; these were also published later.

By the initiative of the Catholic theologian Dr Erich Kellner, there came into being in the 1950s the 'Paulusgesellschaft', a loose association of natural scientists and academics, which first met in order to combat the alienation between science and faith, but then turned to problems of wider public interest and in the 1960 began the dialogue with Marxists. From 1958 Karl Rahner also took an active part in these conferences, soon along with Johann Baptist Metz.

Critical and controversial areas not only of science on an interdisciplinary level but also of contemporary public life were discussed in all three groups. Rahner impressed his conversation partners with the ease with which, while maintaining his standpoint as a member of the Christian church, he could understand another position from within, identify views held in common, indicate the justifications for and limits of pluralism, and above all avoid false alternatives. Even at that time those with marked political interests put up defences against Rahner's openness in practising criticism primarily as self-criticism in his own camp and rejecting the building of barricades. They saw him as a left-wing Catholic, a view which to begin with was not connected with any political option but represented critical detachment from his own system, a concern for renewal and openness to others.

Schriften zur Theologie/*Theological Explorations* and *Mission and Grace*

The collection of the scattered published articles of Karl Rahner was first suggested by the Zurich student pastor Richard Gutzwiller SJ (1896-1958). After making soundings without success among German Catholic publishers, in 1953 (also at the suggestion of the Swiss Jesuit Fr Gutzwiller) Rahner found that Dr Oscar Bettschart of Benziger Verlag in Einsiedeln (later in Zurich) was prepared to support him.[102] As Bettschart himself said, he wanted to make some contribution towards the renewal of theology in the German sphere. Through the republication of the articles, Rahner wanted to see that they had a wider audience, well aware that young theologians needed some impetus to continue their theology and in so doing to remain faithful to their tradition. First of all two volumes were planned, one with articles on specialist theology and one with articles on spirituality. This then became two strictly theological volumes and a third containing articles on spirituality. For technical publishing reasons it appeared under the flexible title *Schriften zur Theologie* ('Writings on Theology') over three years: 1954, 1955 and 1956. Reception of the articles was much more favourable than either author or publisher expected: over the years each sold more than 16,000 copies.

Articles for the fourth volume were collected in 1960; perhaps in them Rahner let his specialist theology retreat even further behind a general, indeed ecumenical, approach orientated on the Council. Despite the special censorship from Rome, which I shall describe later, Volume V could appear in 1962; the articles in it, like those in volume VI (1965), are strongly if not exclusively governed by questions discussed in the context of the Council. Like Vol.III, Vol. VII (1966) contains spiritual articles, including the very short ones which had mounted up since Vol. III. Volume VIII (1967), the longest of the volumes, gathers up contributions on the discussions and dialogues sparked off by the Council: it shows Rahner in conversation with Marxists ('Christian Humanism') and natural scientists ('The experiment man'). This volume and Vol. IX (1970) are a particularly impressive reflection of Rahner's capacity for learning; specifically they show how he took up the political theology of J.B.Metz in a positive way. Volume IX even more markedly serves the renewal of theology in important questions like conversation with the 'world'. This 'return' to theology and to the organization of theology and the function of philosophy in theology comes out even more clearly in Vol.X (1972). Volume XI (1973) brings together Rahner's articles on the history of penance and penitential practice. In Vol.XII (1975) the concentration is on ultimate and radical problems: experience and the hiddenness and incomprehensibility of God, the experience of Jesus Christ, the possibility for a foundation of faith today – and the urgent new ecumenical questions. These themes are taken further in Vol.XIII (1978) and deeper answers to them are sought. By contrast, Vol.XIV (1980) is exclusively concerned with life in the church; it shows Rahner as a theologian deeply concerned for the future of the church. In Vol.XV (1983) Rahner takes further concerns for a contemporary foundation for faith in the light of the questions raised by the natural sciences and atheism; he focusses more clearly than before on the theme of redemption and considers the virtues that are particularly needed today; here he makes an extended contribution to the courage to be active for peace, which an uncompromising rejection of atomic weapons. Volume XVI (1984) contains contributions on the humanizing of society and is then devoted to the future of the church, piety specifically within the church, and the sacraments; it is a volume with a particularly Catholic stamp. In German the sixteen volumes amount to more than 8000 printed pages...

Rahner's volunteer helpers, later his university assistants and collaborators from the Order, gave him a good deal of technical help in preparing the original lectures, first to be printed as articles and then for the *Schriften*. They were Adolf Darlap and Friedrich Korte in Innsbruck, Karl Lehmann and Jorg Splett in Munich, Elmar Klinger, Leo Karter, Kuno Füssel and Heribert Woestmann in Münster, Karl-Heinz Neufeld and Roman Bleistein in Munich and in the later period in Munich and Innsbruck the indefatigable Paul Imhof.

Thus because of the unitary oversight, I was remote from the decisive and intensively productive years of the 1950s. Rahner had excluded the themes relating strictly to church praxis from the first three volumes, although since his article on the pastor in 1943 he had written a good deal on it. In 1959 Rahner gladly collected together for Dr Walter Strolz, at that time the reader of Tyrolia Verlag in Innsbruck, the material for the volume *Sendung und Gnade. Beiträge zur Pastoraltheologie* (ET *Mission and Grace*, London 1963-66, three vols.), which was 561 pages long. The volume begins with a fundamental analysis, a theological interpretation of the position of Christians in the modern world; it then turns to the basic theological questions of pastoral care. It contains articles on ministries and 'states' in the church, already with an eye to the Council, goes into a variety of practical themes (like the railway station mission, pastoral care in prisons, parish libraries and so on) and ends with contributions on the piety of pastoral care. The theological foundation of these articles is so strong that they would also have fitted well into the *Schriften zur Theologie*, just as that series also contains numerous articles which document Rahner's major ideas for church praxis and his pastoral inventiveness. Both this volume and the *Schriften*, or at least selections from them, were translated into the most important European languages: English (the *Schriften* under the title *Theological Explorations* – for a parallel list of German and English volumes see the bibliography), Spanish, Italian and Dutch. *Mission and Grace* attracted much more attention and met with a much wider response. The volume was even read by bishops during the Council.

Lexicon work

In 1955 Rahner allowed Herder Verlag in Freiburg im Breisgau to persuade him to become editor of the *Lexikon für Theologie und Kirche* (*LTK*). Whereas the other editor, Josef Höfer, above all served as adviser and protector, not least thanks to his good connections with Rome, Rahner had to take on more of the burden of scholarly organization. He promised Herder Verlag that from 1 February 1956 onwards he would devote half his working time to *LTK*. In view of the highly respected predecessor of the lexicon, the old *LTK*, which had appeared in an edition of 15,000 copies between 1930 and 1938, Rahner planned that this lexicographical work, too, should be a substantial contribution to the renewal of theology, to a further break-through beyond the limitations which neo-scholasticism inevitably imposed.

Since *LTK* was addressed above all to the clergy, and was to be used in theological education, the church authorities kept particuarly sharp eyes on the growth of the work. The old Bishop of Regensburg, M.Buchberger, as editor of the earlier edition, and indeed of the predecessor of *LTK*, had a legally guaranteed right to be involved. He was asked to take on the 'protectorate' of the new *LTK* along with E.Seiterich, Archbishop of Freiburg, originally a fundamental theologian and formerly a professor in Freiburg. Both bishops took on the function of protectors only on condition that they could have an absolute right of veto on any article. In the preliminary discussions Rahner struggled with both bishops for the rights of a renewed theology. It was agreed that *LTK* should not provide a place for 'avant-garde experiments'; it was primarily to present the *doctrina recepta et communis* (generally accepted teaching) thoroughly and accurately; in addition, however, it might also seek to arouse stimulating and attractive understanding of new questions.

Adolf Darlap was given the responsibility of calculating how long individual articles in the new lexicon needed to be, the terminology to be used in dogmatics and the basic editorial rules. The editorial group was formed in March 1956; at first it consisted of three members, supported by a staff of professional advisers, reputable teachers, who had to propose authors for the articles from the individual disciplines and approve the manuscripts. Darlap left the editorial group in 1958 to pursue his own academic interests. In his place I represented Karl Rahner's interests in the editorial work from 1958 to 1968.

Not least thanks to an enormous effort by Rahner, who approved all the more important and longer articles in manuscript, often improved them throughout and even read the proofs line by line, the planned ten volumes, with 30,000 articles by over 2000 authors, could appear between 1957 and 1965 (the index volume which followed and the three volumes on the Second Vatican Council were not a burden to Rahner in the same way). Karl Rahner in no way planned that *LTK* should be a platform for his theology. He was concerned for the advancement of theology as a whole and under its many aspects. There were plenty of attacks, especially in the first phases of the new lexicon. In the situation of the church at that time they were much more threatening than today, as for example when Archbishop Buchberger criticized the 'existentialist' language of some articles, or Augustine Bea SJ noted with amazement in *Osservatore Romano* that Volume I also contained topics which did not belong to the generally accepted and assured teaching of the church. *LTK* twice went through crises which cast doubts on its whole future, first because of Rahner's article on 'Eschatology' in Vol. III and again because of the article on Jesus Christ written by A. Vögtle in Vol. V. Rahner always encouraged the editors. To give just one example, he wrote to me on 2 December 1959: 'Let's keep going, stay together. We're both unselfishly serving the cause. For *LTK* is an orderly thing. If we remember what is attainable at present and the substantial progress that we have already made, then with

LTK as it is we are not so far behind the mark.' The reason why in the end Rahner wrote a relatively large number of articles himself, and often had to write under considerable pressure of time, was that there were not enough dogmatic theologians then. I can remember a situation in January 1959 when Vol. III was already going to the printer. The adviser on dogmatic theology, M.Schmaus, had himself undertaken important articles for this volume – and then declined at short notice. So Rahner somehow had to get the article on 'Dogma', 'Dogmatics', 'Trinity' and 'Purgatory' from somewhere. The publishing firm, whose lexico-graphical institute was under the dynamic direction of Oscar Köhler, pressed inexorably, especially as the production costs of *LTK* were to a large degree subsidized by German and Austrian bishops and they were responsible to them.

Through these efforts over *LTK* Karl Rahner had come to enjoy lexicon work. A lexicon as a whole gave him the feeling that he was dealing with everything that was important to him. Nevertheless, there was also the opportunity to attend to details and relate the details to the whole. So it came about that he had already begun to think of a new lexicon before *LTK* had reached half its size. In 1961, with Adolf Darlap, he planned a three-volume lexicon which later in fact appeared in four volumes: *Sacramentum Mundi*. He himself described the difference between the two Lexicons in the Preface to Volume I as follows:

> This lexicon seeks to present a *summa* of theological knowledge in alphabetical order, and therefore immediately acccesible, to contemporary people with open minds (both clergy and laity) for them to reflect on in connection with their faith and work. While usually one expects to get from a lexicon something that one does not want to remember permanently, here the opposite is the case: in principle this lexicon seeks to present what the believer should have permanently and vividly at his disposal for giving an account of his faith with the promise assumed in it (I Peter 3.15).

The preparations were long-drawn-out because this lexicon was to have a basically international stamp, while the principle in *LTK* was only to use foreign experts where none were available at home. For the new lexicon Darlap set up an office near Rahner, from March 1962 in Sillgasse, Innsbruck, and later in Munich.

When *Sacramentum Mundi* appeared between 1967 and 1969, it came out in six languages: in English, French, Spanish, Italian, Dutch and German editions, each entrusted to an editor with a substantial reputation in his field: the German edition was supervised by Karl Rahner and Adolf Darlap. From 1972 Herder Verlag utilized the theological substance of Rahner's lexicon work, above all from *Sacramentum Mundi*, in the eight volumes of *Herders Theologische Taschenlexikon* ('Herder's Theological Pocket Lexicon').

We used the summer holidays of 1961, which Rahner spent working on *LTK* in Freiburg, also to write the *Kleine theologische Wörterbuch* (ET *Concise Theological Dictionary*, Burns and Oates 1965). First of all I took A-K and Rahner took L-Z, and then we exchanged manuscripts so that each corrected the other. Of course the whole work was deliberately within the horizons of Rahner's theology, just as the model by which we were stimulated, the *Kleine Philosophische Wörterbuch*, was within the horizons of the philosophy of Max Müller, helped on by Alois Halder. Rahner lovingly called the *Kleine theologische Wörterbuch* the 'little lexicon', using the diminutive form; it was always especially close to his heart. He once wrote to me that one loves the smallest child most. It was a quite unexpected success. Together with the new version which we undertook in the summer of 1975 with the help of Kuno Füssel, and which appeared in 1976 as the tenth edition (the English translation appeared as a second edition in 1983), the German edition alone sold more than 140,000 copies; in addition to the English, there were translations into French, Italian, Dutch, Spanish and Hungarian. Today we should probable look at this lexicon activity more soberly than we did at that time. Today even the best lexicons are largely unused because people with open minds and even students of theology no longer know in what entries they will find particular problems discussed. In advanced old age Rahner also saw that, when he once again involved himself in a project for an encyclopaedia published by Herder Verlag. *Christlicher Glaube in moderner Gesellschaft* ('Christian Faith in Modern Society. An encyclopaedic library in 30 volumes'), edited by F.Böckle, F.-X. Kaufmann, K.Rahner and B.Welter (Freiburg im Breisgau 1980-1983), is no longer alphabetical, but is constructed like a collection of articles.

Quaestiones Disputatae

Even before the war, Karl Rahner and others discussed the need for a series of books on Catholic theology which would indicate that some questions which had long been thought settled are in fact still open, that public discussion can bring out new aspects of a problem, and that even today there is progress in theology. This idea took tangible form in Rahner's years of intensive work in Innsbruck. At an earlier stage he had made contact with the New Testament scholar Heinrich Schlier (1900-1978), a friend of Rudolf Bultmann and pupil of Bultmann, Karl Barth and Martin Heidegger, who had gone over to the Catholic church. He felt him at that time to be an important conversation partner. Schlier was thoroughly familiar with historical-critical scholarship, but he was enough of a philosopher to ask questions about pre-understanding and the main interests of each particular historical discipline. He was very familiar with both Protestant and Catholic dogmatics, and took mere exegesis further so that it became real biblical theology. On 27 June 1956 a decisive conversation took place in which Schlier agreed to edit with Rahner a new series, *Quaestiones Disputatae*, which had been suggested by Robert Scherer, and in it to be responsible for all the biblical questions. The series began to appear in 1958. In the preface to the first volume Rahner wrote:

> There could be room in this series for all that a person seeks to clarify as a Christian, in order to be a better Christian, provided that such clarification is carried out with the objectivity and conceptual strictness which makes reflection a scholarly investigation. If we keep the extent of each individual investigation within reasonable limits, we may perhaps also hope that despite their technical character, these discussions may find a rather wider readership than the professionals. If they also help to bring priests working in the pastorate into a really lively association with theology, and possibly give some ideas to the much-cited lay person with his often urgent theological questions, we would be far more pleased than simply to have our theological learning recognized.

Eight of Karl Rahner's own books were published in this series, and he was co-author of a further eight. A look at the titles is significant: *Über die Schriftinspiration* ('On the Inspiration of Scripture', 1958); *Zur Theologie des Todes* (1958, ET *On the Theology of Death*, 1961); *Visionen und Prophezeiung* (1958, ET *Visions and Prophecies*, 1963); *Das Dynamische in der Kirche* (ET *The Dynamic Element in the Church*, 1964); *Kirche und Sakramente* (1960, ET *Church and Sacraments*, 1964); *Episkopat und Primat* (1961, ET *Episcopacy and Primacy*, with J.Ratzinger, 1964, dedicated to Cardinal Döpfner); *Das Problem der Hominisation* (1961, ET *Hominization*, with P.Overhage, 1961); *Diaconia in Christo. Über die Erneuerung des Diakonats* ('Diaconia in Christo. On the Renewal of the Diaconate', a collection edited by Rahner and myself and dedicated to Cardinals Wyszyński and König, 1962); *Offenbarung und Überlieferung* (1965, ET *Revelation and Tradition*, 1966, with J.Ratzinger); *Die vielen Messen und das eine Opfer* (new edition by A.Haussling, 1966, ET *The Celebration of the Eucharist*, 1968); *Zur Reform des Theologiestudiums* ('On the Reform of the Study of Theology', 1969); an excursus on original sin and monogenism in K.H.Weger, *Theologie der Erbsünde* ('Theology of Original Sin', 1970); *Zum Problem Unfehlbarkeit* ('On the Problem of Infallibility', a collection with fifteen contributors, edited by Rahner, 1971); *Christologie – systematisch und exegetisch* (1972, ET *A New Christology*, with W.Thüsing, 1972); *Vorfragen zu einem ökumenischen Amtsverständnis* ('Preliminary Questions on an Ecumenical Understanding of the Ministry', 1974); *Einigung der Kirchen – reale Möglichkeit* (1983, ET *Unity of the Churches – An Actual Possibility*, with H.Fries, 1985).

We can see from the titles that first of all more loosening up and movement was to be introduced into the 'Pian' period. Then with *Church and Sacraments* there begins a theme which is already connected with the Council. In the time immediately before the Council and during the first periods of the Council it was important to publish as much as possible on questions which were related to the Council's understanding of itself, on themes which were to be discussed or were deliberately not to be discussed. Relevant publications had a great influence on what happened at the Council. In Freiburg im Breisgau the publisher Dr Theophil Herder-Dorneich declared his readiness to contribute everything in his power to literature related to the Council. In the series *Quaestiones Disputatae* he also encouraged titles which could not *a priori* be expected to have a wide readership. This included our book *Diaconia in Christo*. In the first place interest had to be attracted to the theme of the renewal of the diaconate, and secondly, at 646 pages its length was a deterrent. Other titles which should be seen in connection with the Council are H.Küng, *Strukturen der Kirche* (ET *Structures of the Church*, 1964), the work by P.Overhage (in conjunction with Rahner) on the problems of hominization and evolution – indeed Rome had prohibited the reading of Teilhard de Chardin and a dogma on monogenism had been considered; the book by J.R.Geiselmann on scripture and tradition (*Schrift und Tradition*); those by Rahner and Ratzinger on episcopacy and primacy, and on revelation and tradition; the titles by J.Heislbetz and H.R.Schlette on non-Christian religions; and finally the work by L.M.Weber in which this Swiss pastoral theologian, who died prematurely, argued for an openness on the part of the church to the chemical and technical possibilities of a humane system of birth control.

The history of *Quaestiones Disputatae* also reflects to some degree the period after the Council. First of all the series was a great success even in terms of books sold: this was a time of great theological interest and revolution within the church. Then it was subjected to criticism: for some it was too cautious, the tempo was too leisurely; for others this kind of serious scholarship was too difficult. After that, interest in theology generally abated: now the quest was for aids to living, introductions to meditation and the like for those 'interested in spirituality'. Some titles were manifestly too peripheral; these included five volumes on the priestly ministry, and even Karl Rahner's book on the ecumenical understanding of the ministry: they did not sell. Theology had retreated into a much smaller but steady circle. Since Vol.51 (1970), lectures of the annual conferences of dogmatic and fundamental theologians had been included in the series in the form of collected volumes, and rather later also those of conferences on the Old and New Testaments; on one occasion even lectures given at a conference of pastoral theologians was published in the series. It was in these conferences that what in the Middle Ages were called Quaestiones Disputatae were discussed again most clearly in a time of theological famine.

Over the time of the Council Karl Rahner took on too much work and too many projects. To relieve himself of some of the burden he asked me to take on the theological editorship of the series; that happened from Vol.19 on (1964). Since then, year by year we worked together on the series and had to sort out some problematical situations. Even with considerable optimism we had never thought that we would be able to assemble more than 100 *Quaestiones Disputatae*. Rahner saw with delight and amazement the success of his ecumenical no.100, written with Heinrich Fries at Innsbruck over the winter – and with equal amazement the criticism by Cardinal Ratzinger who described what had been written as 'a masterpiece of theological acrobatics which unfortunately does not stand the test of reality', and as passing over the question of truth 'by means of a few dealings in church politics'. Our last theological contact shortly before Rahner's death was over no. 101, a collection on contemporary questions relating to the doctrine of the Trinity.

The *Handbook of Pastoral Theology*

In the light of what has been said so far it must have become clear that Karl Rahner was deeply involved in serving people in the church, in church praxis and in the discipline of pastoral theology. He also understood his own activity as a dogmatic theologian primarily in terms of such practical service and as a service to those involved in praxis. In 1959 he had produced his work *Mission and Grace*, which was about pastoral theology, so it was natural that in planning its theological handbooks Herder Verlag should have had the idea of asking Karl Rahner for his ideas about a *Handbook of Pastoral Theology*. That was in 1960. Rahner threw himself into the task with his distinctive energy and vigour. Fortunately he had given a pupil and friend, Heinz Schuster, as a dissertation theme, 'Practical theology as an academic theological doctrine of the realization of the church called for at any particular time'. He involved him as a collaborator and later as editor of the *Handbook*. To begin with, some of those involved feared that if Rahner appeared in a leading role in this connection, there would be resistance from professional pastoral theologians and other groups. But such considerations went the same way as those over *LTK*; in the end there was no one among the prominent people of the time prepared to take on the burden of work. Rahner, who was convinced that the church needed such a handbook, took over the editorial direction - it was heavy work.

Karl Rahner's conception of pastoral theology or − as he preferred to say − practical theology was extremely demanding. The *Handbook* was to cover two enormous areas: first, it was to show how the church had come to have its present form, and secondly, it was to show in detail what the church should really be about today (what is 'historically appropriate'). This view came up against vigorous resistance from respected pastoral theologians, above all F.X.Arnold of Tübingen and J.M.Reuss, the suffragan bishop of Mainz. They thought that this conception was too dangerous for younger theologians. The younger theologians should not study church strategy, but simply pastoral work. They should not themselves experiment in planning, but humbly receive instructions.

In many round-table meetings, beginning with a first discussion in Freiburg on 21 November 1960, Rahner sought to overcome the opposition and win co-editors from among the pastoral theologians. Finally he succeeded: F.X.Arnold, F.Klostermann, V.Schurr and L.M.Weber declared themselves ready to share the responsibility. The presence of Klostermann and Weber meant that the involvement of Austria and Switzerland was also secured. With Robert Scherer of Herder Verlag and Heinz Schuster, Rahner attempted to gain support for the new project abroad, above all first in France. A meeting with distinguished Dominicans there − M.D.Chenu, A.M.Henry and P.A.Liégé − in April 1961 got nowhere. The differences between the French and the Germans were too great: in mentality, in delight in church organization, in reflective academic language; in addition the French Dominicans were defensive towards Rahner. Thus the new *Handbook* predominantly represented the German-speaking world, though later it was also translated into other languages.

Volumes I-IV appeared in five part-volumes between 1964 and 1969; then in 1972 there followed a lexicon which went with them, edited by F.Klostermann, K.Rahner and H.Schild, and with 279 contributors. Rahner himself had written important articles in the *Handbook*: on the foundation of pastoral theology as practical theology, the basic nature of the church, the presence of the truth and love of God, the presence of God's communication of himself; on the vehicles of the church's self-realization, the whole church as subject, ministry and charisma, the members of the hierarchy, the sacraments (Vol.I); also, among others, on theological anthropology, the situation of the church in the present (II.1); mission, church and world (II.2); times of life (III); and the sacrament of penance and priestly training (Vol.IV).

The pastoral theologians were rather slow in taking up Rahner's suggestions. Norbert Mette began a constructive conversation with him. In the year of Rahner's death, two books appeared on practical theology in which his voice can again be heard: Walbert Bühlmann, *Weltkirche* ('World Church'), Graz 1984, with an article by Karl Rahner on 'Perspectives of Pastoral Care in the Future', and Paul.M.Zulehner, *'Denn du kommst unserem Tun mit deiner Gnade zuvor'* ('For you anticipate our action with your grace', Düsseldorf 1984), a conversation with Karl Rahner on the theology of pastoral care today.

Further initiatives, *Concilium* and *Mysterium Salutis*

What I have described so far is by no means all that could be said about Karl Rahner's activity in the most productive phase of his life. His relations with Herder Verlag, with Robert Scherer, led to yet other plans being realized there which had been suggested by the Munich group in 1938, projects in which Rahner only provided a stimulus and was not active as a collaborator. Also at his suggestion there came into being, in particular, the *Theologische Kommentar zum Neuen Testament*, which has been appearing since 1953, and the *Handbuch der Dogmengeschichte*, which has been appearing in fascicles since 1951. Both were intended to meet an urgent need for Catholic theology to catch up.

I should also mention projects in which Rahner was involved beyond the first stages of planning. Of all foreign publishers, Paul Brand from Ankeveen in Holland was the first who personally had access to Rahner's thought; at a very early stage he arranged translations of Rahner texts into Dutch, invited Rahner to his home at Hilversum and took a lively part in Rahner's great projects. Around this publisher there gathered the group of theologians who at the time of the Council brought into being the international theological journal *Concilium*. The journal was supported by a foundation in Hilversum and supervised by a general secretariat. Direction of the content lay with an editorial committee and was divided among individual sections. Right up to his death Karl Rahner was a member of the editorial committee and took part in its planning sessions as often as he could. He also joined in the public appeals made by *Concilium* theologians, e.g. for free and unhindered theological work. With E.Schillebeeckx he edited the first number in 1965. However, he did not personally direct the section on dogmatics, but the section on pastoral theology (with Heinz Schuster as second director). In the jubilee volume of December 1983, 'Twenty Years of *Concilium* – Retrospect and Prospect', Rahner expressed his solidarity with this journal: 'For my part I believe that *Concilium* has no need to be ashamed of its past, but, on the contrary, can be grateful to God and to the men and women who have kept this journal going. My wish is that *Concilium* will live on bravely and joyfully and continue to carry out its task "in season and out of season".'[103] At a truly international level the journal addressed itself to the specific questions of contemporary people; that is, it did not pass over either moral problems or the threat to faith posed by the questionable features of church praxis: it bears witness to something of Rahner's antipathy to window dressing. Rahner always also supported the impulses of Johann Baptist Metz to make the journal the voice of the so-called Third World. *Concilium* became the exponent of a particular theological position and movement in the church at the latest by 1972, when a group around Hans Urs von Balthasar with J.Ratzinger, K.Lehmann, the politician H.Maier, and others founded their own *Internationale katholische Zeitschrift*, which was subsidized by the bishops.

O. Bettschart of Benziger Verlag took up the idea put forward by Karl Rahner in the first volume of his *Schriften* about the need to construct a new dogmatics. Experiences with the last German-speaking dogmatic theologians had shown that in view of the wealth of theological insights from different disciplines to be incorporated, it was no longer possible for an individual theologian to write a whole *Dogmatics*. An attempt to implement Rahner's outline could therefore only be made through international teamwork. Rahner allowed himself to be persuaded by Bettschart to do some preliminary thinking and join in the planning. From 1958 the Swiss theologians Johannes Feiner and Magnus Löhrer OSB have been involved in the work as editors.

They, too, often went to Rahner for advice. The new dogmatics appeared between 1965 and 1976 in five volumes (seven part-volumes) with the title *Mysterium Salutis* and was also immediately translated into other European languages. Karl Rahner himself wrote the contributions on kerygma and dogma (with K.Lehmann I, 622-703), the historicity of mediation (with K.Lehmann, I, 727-82), the triune God as the transcendent primal ground of salvation history (II, 317-97), fundamental considerations on anthropology and protology in the framework of theology (II, 406-20), *prolixitas mortis* (V, 466-72) and 'Dying seen in the light of death' (V, 473-92). A supplementary volume which appeared in 1981 contains a survey by M.Löhrer of the origins of this great work (13-37), in which Rahner's share in the creation of the work is also acknowledged.

10 Difficulties

Karl Rahner was a troublesome person right up to his death. He was outspoken to the point of rudeness, and with a creative imagination he had new ideas which he wanted to see discussed. He loved the church above all else and would never have allowed it to be second to friendship with a person. However, he wanted to help people, even if principles and regulations were violated as a result. He hated pious affectation, but self-righteous certainty even more. He was a freedom-loving man and could discover areas of freedom even where the official line had long regarded everything as regulated or prohibited.

So from the first post-war years onwards he had made himself unpopular in official church circles. Younger men today no longer know the background against which Rahner's early and sharp criticism of the church is to be seen. Immediately after the war, Christians with any degree of awareness had been seized by a serious concern for renewal, a new beginning. In their eyes this included a reworking of the past, the will to face guilt, even the church's share of guilt in the rise of barbarity. An unmistakable signal in Germany was Ida Friederike Görres' letter on the church which was published in the newly founded *Frankfurter Heften* (8, 1946), in which she used the derogatory term 'clerical fascism'

for the unfeeling attitude which is concerned only for the reputation of the church's ministry and its power. Karl Rahner wanted
to take up the justified concerns of this respected Catholic writer
– later she lived in the same home as Rahner's mother, and he
often met her - but he also saw the danger that criticism of the
church might turn into a complete rejection of the church. He
wanted to do justice to both criticism and rescuing the church.

There were many in office who thought that a new beginning
was quite superfluous. For them the church was the only authority
to have remained intact in the Nazi barbarism, and they proudly
flaunted this view. They thought that nothing was necessary for
rebuilding other than strict, uncritical obedience towards the
hierarchy. Regional authorities were scandalized at what Rahner
said in public, from 'Kirche der Sünder' ('Church of Sinners',
1947) through the 'Theologische Deutung der Position des
Christen in der modernen Welt' ('Theological Interpretation of
the Position of Christians in the Modern World', 1954) to 'Löscht
den Geist nicht aus' ('Do not Stifle the Spirit', 1962). Bishops
approached Rahner's superiors in the Order to make known their
discontent and obtained partial prohibitions against him, so that
Rahner could no longer speak on certain themes (e.g. hot issues
like the confessional school).[104] Church organizers were given
hints to stop inviting Rahner. To begin with, this had no reper-
cussions for Rahner in Rome.

The *Mariology*

In 1951 a very large manuscript by Rahner did not receive from
the Order the permission required for it to be printed. Karl
Rahner had written 393 closely typed pages on 'Problems of
Contemporary Mariology' which he completed on 13 June 1951
and submitted to the usual censorship of the Order. Rahner's
brother Hugo and his colleague Franz Lakner were appointed
censors. The latter did not feel capable of judging the text. The
superiors in the Order did not follow Rahner's recommendation
that the Frankfurt Jesuit J.Beumer, who was ready to help, should
be accepted as second censor, but passed the matter on to the
leaders of the Order in Rome. These appointed the fundamental
theologian E.Dhanis SJ of the Gregorian University as censor, and

he recommended that permission to print should be refused. So that is what happened.[105]

After an introduction the manuscript contains four long chapters and an excursus. The first part is concerned with the question of the development of dogmas and the origin of new dogmas generally. The second describes the history of the doctrine that Mary was taken up into heaven body and soul, a doctrine which can be found for the first time in legends of the fifth century. Rahner follows the history of this doctrine, in the Eastern churches as well, and offers an interpretation of the papal bull which contains the new dogma promulgated in 1950 by Pius XII concerning the Assumption of Mary. The third part contains Rahner's theology on this dogma. Here is an attempt to affirm the dogma fully and completely, and yet to tone down several points in a way which is called for in view of the scantiness of the sources, the great lack of faith in the twentieth century and the explosion caused in the ecumenical sphere. Rahner attempts to think in terms of a total view of man, though governed by the spirit, in the light of the possibility of the total consummation of man in death, including a bodily consummation – now, and that means not just at the last day. In short, to put it another way, according to this view Mary would not be an individual case, but every dead person would be taken up by God into a state of consummation which also involved corporeality – though in an inconceivable and utterly changed form. This idea of a 'resurrection in death' is common today among many theologians, and not everyone is aware that Rahner is its author. Here Rahner also looks for biblical support, in the statement in Matt.27.52f. that after the death of Jesus many dead were raised up with their bodies. Rahner is of course concerned with Mary, but he clearly indicates the positive implications for all human beings to be found in this reference in dogma to the corporeality of humanity and our consummation. That is what he is concerned with in the fourth chapter, in which he also seeks to tone down and relativize objections to the new dogma. The excursus is concerned with the theology of death; here Rahner draws further consequences from his idea of consummation in death which he compares with the previous unsatisfactory idea of a mere continued existence of the isolated soul in death.

The book contains numerous phrases of Rahner's in which he

expresses his objections vigorously, not to the content of the dogma but to the time of its promulgation, its 'necessity'. Rahner never attacked the Marian piety of Pius XII, but he would have preferred the Pope to keep it private and not make it binding on the church. The fact that in this connection Rahner described the 'messenger of the truth of God' as possibly a 'suspiciously pious sheep or a fiery zealot' (4) must have shocked the one Roman censor.

The book with its reflections on dogma and theological anthropology could have provided important impulses – though Rahner presented these later under other titles. It would have given counsel and help to many people, above all in Central Europe, who had been scandalized by the new dogma. But apart from the *Theology of Death*, it still remains unpublished to this day. When Rahner moved from Innsbruck to Munich he had hopes of finding young collaborators who would have worked over the two manuscripts on Mariology and the sacrament of penance for him. At least the publications of the previous ten years would have had to be incorporated. Rahner did not find these collaborators.

Concelebration

In 1949 Rahner had written a long article with the title 'Die vielen Messen und das eine Opfer' ('The Many Masses and the One Sacrifice', which appeared as a pamphlet in 1951). In it he discussed a theme which is no longer current today, even among theologians: are the 'fruits of the mass', the signs of honour towards God, multiplied by the number of eucharists celebrated? If not, what does that mean for the frequency and form of the mass? Could many priests concelebrate? But in such a way that this would not be many masses of many priests, but just one mass? And what is the relationship between the masses celebrated by the church and the one sacrifice that they make present, the event on the cross? The traditional doctrine argued for a multiplication of the fruits of the mass, and thus for the largest possible number of masses, at the same time having the idea that in this way more money would also come in for the masses (stipends). Rahner demolished the traditional arguments. In 1954 Pius XII in a public statement rejected parts of Rahner's statements, but without mentioning Rahner's name. Thereupon the authorities of the faith, the so-called Holy Office, forbade Rahner to speak in future on the theme of concelebration. After the Council Rahner took the opportunity at a private audience with Paul VI to say to the Pope, 'Look, Holy Father, ten years ago the Holy Office forbade me to say anything about concelebration, and today even you are concelebrating.' Telling the story, Rahner went on to say, 'He then laughed very gently and said, "Est tempus flendi, est tempus ridendi" ' (there is a time for weeping and a time for laughing).[106] By this quotation from the Old Testament book of Koheleth he probably meant to indicate that even the measures of an authority of the faith did not last for ever.

The 'virgin birth'

In 1960 Rahner had written an article in which he had questioned the Catholic doctrine of the *virginitas in partu,* the doctrine that Mary had remained a virgin perpetually after the birth of Jesus. He attempted to interpret this doctrine, communicated in the time-honoured formulas of the ever-virgin Mary mother of God, in his 'typical' manner. He sought the 'nucleus' of the statement and attempted with all his energy to maintain this nucleus; he enquired into the presentation and the additions to this nucleus, into what was eternally valid in the historically conditioned statement, and sought to make it clear why people of all ages have inevitably to make use of such additions in order to be able to express the 'substance itself'. Now the intention of all the ancient writers who had said anything about the virginity of Mary was certainly not to express the biological or anatomical aspects. So Rahner asked what the nucleus of 'virginity' 'really' is. He came up with a religious and theological content: a person is virgin who is wholly orientated on the fulfilment of the will of God, who is 'at God's disposal'. Of course in this deeper sense married people, too, can be virgin. With this solution Rahner succeeded in solving all the problems which arise from the mention in the Bible of the brothers of Jesus.

This article caused serious disturbances in Roman circles. Rumours were circulated that now steps would really be taken against Rahner. They caused Cardinal Julius Döpfner, who had alway shown Rahner signs of appreciation and sympathy, to intercede for him with John XXIII in an audience of 24 January

1961. The consequence of this intervention was that not only were no proceedings set in motion, but on 22 March 1961 he was nominated by John XXIII as the *consultor* (adviser) of the Council's preparatory commission on the discipline of the sacraments.[107] That was a highly official 'settlement'. Still, Rahner had come under suspicion to such a degree that the Jesuit Gregorian University, after first inviting him, then cancelled the invitation.

Preliminary censorship

Without prior warning or previous new rumours, on 7 June 1962 Rahner's superiors in the Order informed him that from now on everything that he wrote had to be submitted to a preliminary censorship in Rome.[108] This measure fitted into the pre-conciliar 'landscape'. Already in the 1950s unpopular theologians, above all in France, had been silenced by Rome. Where they were members of Orders, the measures were particularly far-reaching: some were even banished to other countries. In the time of Pope John XXIII the Pontifical Biblical Institute was above all the focal point of such attacks. Rahner's feeling was that this time there was no specific occasion for the measure (though his speech 'Do not Stifle the Spirit' at the Austrian Catholics' Day in Salzburg on 1 June 1962 had again been a cause for offence for those who wanted to be offended; the time was too short for a Roman measure which had to follow protocol), but that they simply wanted to 'stop his mouth', like those of others, before the Council, and make it impossible for him to take part in the Council, since in this way he had been 'previously punished' by the church. Rahner alerted Cardinals König and Döpfner, who were well disposed to him, and his friends Bishop Volk and Prelate Höfer in Rome. A few days later König spoke with John XXIII and asked for protection for Rahner. On 23 June Rahner himself went to Rome for a day to see the Jesuit General; the latter was well disposed, but said that he was only a messenger for the Holy Office: neither Rahner nor the Jesuit General were given reasons for the preliminary censorship. Rahner was given permission to bring out Vol.V of the *Schriften*, since the writings collected in it had already been through the censor and the preliminary censorship was not meant to be retrospective. At the end of June, Cardinals Döpfner, König and Frings, who had been persuaded by Volk, sent a written document to the Pope asking for this preliminary censorship to be lifted. König was entrusted with the composition of the text. The matter could not be kept secret. When it was even broadcast on the radio that Rahner was prohibited from writing and speaking, Dr E.Kellner of the Paulus Gesellschaft started a petition among the members and friends of the Gesellschaft. He collected about 250 signatures, including very many university scientists. Professor Paul Martini, physician to Chancellor Adenauer, informed him about the action and persuaded him to see that the petition was handed over to the Pope through diplomatic channels and with Adenauer's own endorsement. H.Schäufele (died 1977), Archbishop of Freiburg, successfully established in Rome that Rahner's article for Vol.VII of *LTK* did not have to go through the preliminary censorship, as he told the editors on 11 September 1962. In August the Pope had said to Cardinal Bea that he would find ways to satisfy the cardinals and Rahner. But nothing happened. Nevertheless in October 1962 John XXIII nominated Rahner a Council theologian (*peritus*), and the Prefect of the Holy Office, Cardinal A.Ottaviani, raised no objections when Cardinal König took Rahner with him to the commission sessions. This work at the Council made Rahner's opponents in Rome familiar with him. In February 1963 Rahner spoke with Ottaviani about his situation during an interval between sessions. Ottaviani explained the preliminary censorship by saying that they wanted to protect Rahner from friends who misunderstood him, and that was a privilege.[109] Rahner replied that he would gladly forego this privilege. On 28 May 1963 the Jesuit General told Rahner that the Holy Office had retreated completely over the matter of the preliminary censorship. He, the general, was alone to appoint Rahner's censors, and he would appoint the ones who had held the position earlier.

From that point on Rahner had no such similar difficulties. In the circles of those who were discontented with the Council and more recent theology there were constantly people who called for administrative measures against him. But he had freedom to the end of his life.

Karl Rahner did not regard the suspicions, machinations and measures directed against him as dispensations of divine providence which had been sent to test his humility and his disposition

towards the church. He never had the impression that the hierarchy had deeper insights than he had. He did not describe those
who brought suffering on others in order to compel compliant
behaviour or silence and thus demonstrate their power in the
church as instruments of God, but, as he wrote in his letter of 26
June 1962 (150 below) as 'terrible bigwigs'. He had only cold
contempt for ministers who found it necessary to listen to rumours
and denunciations, who made use of a system of informers and
tale-bearers. How often he said to me, in conversations or in
letters, right down to the last years of his life: 'Only those whom
you respect can hurt you.' However, his feeling for the church
was so strong that despite all his bad experiences he never
identified those who held power with the church as a whole: they
should not and would not force him out of the church.

11   The Council and Rahner's International
     Reputation

On 25 January 1959 John XXIII made a public announcement of
his plan to summon a council. Of course, the question now arose
as to which theologians would be involved in this council and in
what way. As a result of his publications and lecture tours, by
that time Karl Rahner had already made himself such a name
outside the German-speaking world that many people interested
in his theology and in the church took it for granted that he would
be involved. On the other hand, in official church circles there
were warnings about 'progressive' theologians and measures
against them. In Rome, Rahner had experienced some of the
difficulties mentioned above. His main opponents there were
known to be the Jesuits Sebastian Tromp and Franz Hürth, the
former a dogmatic theologian and the latter a moral theologian
at the Gregorian Institute; both were *consultores* (advisers) to the
Holy Office. The Prefect of the Holy Office, Cardinal Ottaviani,
and its assessor, Archbishop P.Parente, were also among Rahner's
opponents.

  On 5 June 1960 John XXIII officially set up the preparatory
organs of the Council: a central commission, ten commissions
and three secretariats. They had to work through about 2000

requests, suggestions and questions which had come in from all over the world: they had to plan the form in which the Council was to be presented. The restoration of the permanent diaconate was one of these requests. The provisional decision lay with the central commission.

Karl Rahner was by disposition very strongly committed to the renewal of the permanent diaconate. He was most impressed by the idealism of the pioneers in it (Hannes Kramer in Freiburg, with whom he spoke for the first time in 1948 about the matter, and Joseph Hornef in Fulda), and he had high hopes that such a reform within the church would bringing about a relaxation of the picture presented by the clergy, so that it became more varied. The new clergy would have to be capable of doing professional secular work and of earning their living, which would avoid the impression of a sacrality remote from the world; moreover they could choose whether or not to marry. Of course Rahner was also always well aware of the burning concerns in missionary lands and in areas like South America which had few priests. He himself discussed the matter publicly for the first time in 1957. After the theme had been assigned to the commission for the discipline of the sacraments, this committee noted that Rahner was so far the only dogmatic theologian who had defined his position over the diaconate. Since problems relating to the sacrament of ordination, authorities and so on had to be considered, the commission needed a dogmatic theologian. The Roman circles who had reservations about Rahner allowed him to join in the preparations for the Council over this limited question. As I have said, John XXIII nominated him adviser to the relevant commission. Rahner was never invited to a session in Rome, but he was asked to send a comment on the renewal of the diaconate, which he had to work out in collaboration with the Yugoslavian archbishop F.Šeper (later Cardinal and Prefect of the Congregation of Faith). This text was included in the preparatory outline (schema) of a decree on the sacrament of ordination which was prepared by the commission during 1961.[110]

In October 1961 Cardinal Franz König asked Rahner to look through the dossiers which the individual commissions had worked out for the central commission and to give him his opinion. In this way Rahner became private adviser to Cardinal König at the Council. He knew the Archbishop of Vienna not just as an Austrian bishop. König had asked Rahner for various articles for a dictionary of religion which had appeared in 1956. Over *LTK*, from the first volume on (1957), König was a knowledgeable and hard-working adviser on religion and the history of religion, and in this capacity was also often in contact with Rahner.

In Spring 1962 Rahner had to give reports in Latin for König on the schemata intended by the central commission for the Council. He was interested above all in the texts from the sphere of dogmatics and moral theology which had to be provided by his opponents Tromp and Hürth: On keeping pure the deposit of faith; on the sources of revelation; on the church; on the blessed Virgin Mary, mother of God and mother of man; on chastity, virginity, marriage and the family; on the moral order. The groups preparing for the Council had the impression that these texts – which simply repeated what had always been said, i.e. above all in the past century, without the slightest concession to the people of the present – had been worked out in such a solid way that the Council could give them its blessing without much trouble and dissolve itself in a very short time. They suggested that what the age needed was a summary, a syllabus, of the current philosophical and theological 'errors'. In this *first phase*, the reaction of those theologians and bishops who did not see things in this way was that it was necessary to hinder what could be hindered. Rahner refused to approve this procedure. Cardinal Döpfner also asked him for the texts prepared for König.

On 11 October 1962 the Council was solemnly opened by John XXIII and its tone set by the comments in which the Pope declared himself against the mere repetition of dogmatic formulae. The Pope wanted to encourage the forces of renewal; he ruled out condemnations. At the end of October Karl Rahner and about 190 other theologians were nominated official *periti*. At first this simply meant that he received a pass with which he was allowed access to the sessions of the Council in St Peter's. There the *periti* sat on a tribune assigned to them which was so narrow that they could hardly make manuscript notes. As the bishops were only making speeches in the *aula* of St Peter's that the *periti* had written for them earlier, Rahner found being on the tribune tedious. He visited the official sessions of the Council only rarely. With his *peritus* pass he was not in any way allowed to take part in the sessions of any of the commissions of the Council.

His real work took place primarily outside the official meetings. He addressed the German-speaking bishops, was invited by the South American bishops, took part in theological meetings of the French and Germans, and so on. After the first discusssion of the content of the schema on liturgy, on 14 November discussion began of the prepared text on the sources of revelation. This was a theme which in various respects occupied a key position in the church and theology. If there was a second 'source' of divine revelation alongside Holy Scripture, namely oral tradition, then there was really nothing in the way of an expansion of the creed, the content of faith; new things could always be discovered in the oral tradition. This also made it impossible to come to an understanding with Christians who based their belief on 'scripture alone'. Rahner had written a Latin counter-opinion. In addition, so that the bishops who remained undecided could see what a contemporary text on revelation might look like, Ratzinger and Rahner composed a schema of their own which was authorized by Cardinal Frings in the name of the German bishops' conference and presented to the other bishops.[111] After a stormy debate it was rejected on 20 November. The opponents of the official schema did not secure the necessary majority, but the minority was so qualified that on 21 November John XXIII withdrew the schema and formed a mixed commission which had to work out a new text. This was the breakthrough; from then on the texts prepared in Rome beforehand were no longer regarded as inviolable.

As the Council went on, the pattern of work repeated itself for Rahner: after the prepared texts on the church and on Mary had been circulated on 23 November and the discussion of that on the church had begun on 1 December, he had again to give an opinion orally and in writing. The experts produced a real flood of paper. Rahner once reported in this phase that with a few willing helpers he had duplicated 50,000 sheets of paper.

On 5 December 1962 his own decisive personal breakthrough began: Cardinal König simply took him into a session of the mixed commission which was directed by Cardinals Ottaviani and Bea with equal rights, and which had to work out the new text on revelation. Ottaviani had the right to exclude Rahner; he did not.[112] This procedure was repeated on 7 December. Subseqently Rahner gained great respect also from theologians on the other side, the Italians and others trained in Rome, as a result of his deep knowledge of the tradition, his sovereign command of Latin and his logical acuteness in argument. He was accepted.

After the end of the first period of the Council on 8 December 1962, the sessions of the commissions continued in individual countries and in Rome. In February 1963 Rahner was officially nominated *peritus* and member of an expert group of seven theologians who had to work out a new text on the church. Work on revelation ran in parallel, and Cardinal König added outlines of a newly planned schema on the church in the modern world. Rahner indefatigably wrote opinions, including one on Mary, for the German and Austrian Bishops' Conferences.

In Autumn 1963 he took part in the conference of a theological group in Malines, Belgium, which had been convened by Cardinal Suenens (6-8 September). Here work was done on a text on the church in the modern world, which was afterwards developed into a schema by the Belgian dogmatic theologian Gerard Philips (1899-1972), secretary of the theological commission of the Council. In this way Rahner became good friends with Philips, and their quiet collaboration was important as the Council proceeded.

In this second phase of the work of the Council a different way was pursued in respect of the new texts, since mere hindrance had proved successful: to keep the texts as 'open' as possible, to say nothing which could lead too quickly to a dogmatic assertion.

In the second period of the Council, which lasted from 29 September to 4 December 1963, there were important consultations and votes in which Rahner played a major part: on 30 September the discussion of the new text on the church and on 29 October the vote on whether a separate dogmatic text should be made on Mary or whether the statements of the Council on Mary should be incorporated into the schema on the church; then on 30 October there was a test vote on five questions relating to the schema on the church, including one on the theme of the diaconate which was so close to Rahner's heart. Rahner took part in a sub-commission which worked on the schema on the church; he turned his attention above all to the collegiality of bishops and their relationship to the Pope, and to the status of local communities. He advised those bishops who – like Cardinal König

– thought it necessary to incorporate statements about Mary into the schema on the church. He also took part in sessions of the commission which worked on the conciliar text on members of Orders. In this *second phase* of the Council the generally agitated and aggressive mood of the first phase gave place to a more rational and peaceful climate – though there were some dramatic controversies as in the 'battle over Mary' – and I think that Rahner made a major contribution towards relaxing the mood. Again he was involved in numerous lectures on the fringe of the Council, including some for the South American bishops and his special friends, the Brazilians. In this period of the session a great public reception for the theologians of *Sacramentum Mundi* was organized with the friend of the new Pope, the Italian dogmatic theologian Carlo Colombo. Now Rahner was also regarded by the other side, in the words of the 'conservative' Mariologist C.Balič OFM, as 'the most powerful man' at the Council.

At home in the first half of 1964 Rahner worked above all on the conciliar texts on the relationship of scripture and tradition (he was also active in the relevant sub-commission in Rome) and on Mary.

The third period of the Council lasted from 14 September to 21 November 1964. Again texts were discussed in connection with which Rahner was in great demand: from 15 September that on the church, from 16 September that on Mary, now chapter VIII of the text on the church, from 30 September that on revelation and from 20 October that on the church in the modern world. Rahner's involvement was significant, particularly on the theme of the inerrancy of scripture (in the schema on revelation) and in setting the basic theological trend and giving an account of the Christian view of man in the text on the church in the modern world. In Rahner's view a *third phase* of the Council had now begun: the very first beginnings – 'a beginning of beginnings', as he also put it – could be traced.

The fourth period of the Council began on 14 September and ended on 8 December 1965. From 21 September onwards there was discussion of the lengthy text on the church in the modern world; the final redactions of numerous documents were under way, and on 9 November Rahner once again came into his own in the *aula* of St Peter's. On this day there was discussion of a new order for indulgences. Here Patriarch Maximus IV Saigh and

Cardinals Alfrink, Döpfner and König represented Rahner's theology of indulgences.[113]

If we survey the sixteen texts which the Second Vatican Council passed and solemnly proclaimed, it is difficult, indeed impossible, at this stage to trace the influence of Karl Rahner in detail. Certainly K.Neufeld is right to say that no trace of Rahner's influence can be found in four texts: on the means of communication, on the eastern churches, on Christian education and – remarkably – on religious freedom.[114] In all the rest, beginning with the constitution on the liturgy, we can see traces of Rahner's theology. Without doubt, Rahner's publications on church and sacraments, episcopacy and primacy, revelation and tradition, the inspiration of scripture and the diaconate were as important for bishops as for conciliar theologians. But Rahner so agreed with the other theologians of the generation concerned for renewal that it cannot be said with certainty that the introduction of a particular passage is to be attributed to him (alone). At a very early stage, in 1947, Rahner had already described the church as a sacrament, i.e. as an effective sign for the salvation of the world. But quite a number of other theologians did the same thing. If the Council took over this view of the church, how could it now be established whether this was as a result of Rahner or of someone else? In the end it does not matter. Rahner worked with incredible persistence for the renewal of the diaconate, and in 1985 there were already 11,223 permanent deacons throughout the world. But who could attribute this success to Rahner alone?

Rahner was active at the Council to the point of exhaustion. He indicated what he himself saw twenty years later as the permanent significance of the Council in Vol. XIV of his *Schriften*.

His work at the Council had two direct consequences. The German-speaking bishops knew that Rahner and I wanted to publish the texts of Vatican II as an appendix to *LTK* with commentaries by experts. They asked Rahner and me to examine critically the existing rough translations and provide a reliable final version. This work took many weeks in the winter of 1965/66; the result was approved by the presidents of the bishops' conferences.

On 28 March 1966 Rahner wrote to me in a letter from Chicago that in the USA he had seen a 794-page paperback edited by Walter M.Abbott SJ containing all the texts of the Council with short introductions and an index. (In his letter there is the remark: 'Incidentally, Cardinal MacIntyre has banned the book as being dangerous for laity in his diocese. That's still the case in America. Although elsewhere things are happening.') Rahner now suggested that Herder paperbacks should do the same thing, especially as the idea was not patented. We carried out this plan after Rahner's return. Rahner wrote a general introduction to the Second Vatican Coucil, and I wrote the introductions to the sixteen conciliar texts; the *Kleine Konzilskompendium* appeared in December 1966. The eighteenth impression was published in 1985.

The move to Munich

An important event took place in the life and activity of Karl Rahner during the period of the Council; he left Innsbruck and went to Munich; he officially gave up dogmatics and changed to the philosophy of religion. Inquiries from the philosophical faculty in Munich as to whether Rahner would like to be the successor to Romano Guardini in the Chair for Christianity and the Philosophy of Religion, which had Guardini's full backing, reached him in February 1963. He felt that the move to a West German university would provide greater protection against hindrances like the Roman censorship measures – in view of the declarations of solidarity which he had received from the scientists of the Paulusgesellschaft; moreover he hoped that there would be more opportunity of easing his burden of work somewhat by a series of younger collaborators; and finally, the climate in Innsbruck was no longer very collegial. So he was very interested, indeed burningly interested, in Munich: he waited impatiently for the call. As a Jesuit he needed the consent of the Order for any move. Though the General had earlier once forbidden Rahner to accept a call to Münster as a dogmatic theologian because he thought Innsbruck more important than Münster, in May 1963 he gave him permission to go to Munich. The call was made in November of the same year and Rahner accepted. He moved to Munich as early as December, but he had agreed that he would only begin lecturing in the summer semester of 1964.

Honours

The date 5 March 1964, Karl Rahner's sixtieth birthday, marked a series of honours given to him which continued unbroken to the end of his life. These attest a wide and deep influence, international recognition and great gratitude from numerous people for Rahner's services.

As early as 1962, Rahner's four earliest pupils (Darlap, Kern, Metz and I) prepared a great Festschrift for this birthday. I asked him what he thought of the idea of a *tabula gratulatoria*, a list of congratulations, being printed in it. He replied: 'I think so: in itself such a *tabula gratulatoria* is not an unreasonable idea. It may impress on the Holy Office and other similar places that if they embark on machinations against me they will offend too many people. And if someone wants to do make one, to that degree I am in favour.'

How important the idea became to him is shown by his reaction when one of his former friends became agitated about this list: 'I am cross about M.M.'s comments on the *tabula gratulatoria*. The man should be more capable of understanding why it can be important for me, indeed very important. It may very soon be that I have to be glad of any moral support. If you like, write to him that he need not join in what is eyewash and a great nonsense' (Letter from Rome, 11 November 1963). And soon afterwards he wrote: 'I'm still most grateful for it. As far as one can foresee anything, I shall still be able to use a stock of prestige. For it is far from the case that my most "dangerous" matters have already been written' (Letter from Rome, 23 November 1963). When the Festschrift *Gott in Welt* ('God in the World') appeared, edited by A.Darlap, W.Kern, J.B.Metz and myself, and was distributed by the publisher Dr Theophil Herder-Dornreich, who had generously supported it, the *tabula gratulatoria* contained more than 900 names from all over the world. It began with fourteen cardinals, two patriarchs and numerous bishops and abbots; it contained the names of Karl Barth, Rudolf Bultmann and other prominent Protestant theologians, of Martin Heidegger, the two Taizé brothers Roger Schutz and Max Thurian, the politician Gustav Heinemann, and those of numerous theological colleagues of Rahner and many natural scientists and academics. The two volumes ran to 1714 pages containing seventy-one contributions on basic philosophical and theological questions, on biblical themes, on the theology of Jesus Christ and the church, on the problem of religions and confessions, on interdisciplinary problems relating to philosophy and theology and the arts and sciences. This was the first time that Karl Rahner's influence had been documented beyond his professional sphere and beyond the German-speaking world, indeed beyond the bounds of his confession.

The honorary doctorate of theology from the Catholic theological faculty of the University of Münster which he received shortly after his birthday marked the beginning of a series of more than a dozen honorary doctorates which were bestowed on him in later life. The mark of honour bestowed on him by the district of the Tyrol was followed by orders of all kinds, including in West Germany in 1970 the Grand Cross of the Order of Merit with Star and Pour le mérite for Science and the Arts. After receiving the Reuchlin prize from the town of Pforzheim in 1965, Rahner was given many prizes by various institutions; his original language was recognized by the Sigmund Freud prize for academic prose awarded by the German Academy for Language and Poetry in 1973. Karl Rahner's self-esteem was not inflated by such honours, but he did have a childlike delight in them. He showed close friends who visited him medals, crosses and documents, though he described them all as a 'circus'. One honour which would have particularly delighted him, because he was attached to his home town of Freiburg, but which he did not receive, was the honorary doctorate of the theological faculty there; however, shortly before his death he learned that the town of Freiburg intended to make him an honorary citizen, and that pleased him.

Further Festschrifts must be included in this survey of honours. One for his seventieth birthday, which Johann Baptist Metz and I had prepared, was turned down by Herder, Benziger and Kösel Verlag because of a contribution by Heinrich Böll. Böll's article attacked with harsh language people in the church who wounded others, singling out in particular those in office. Cardinal Döpfner was prepared to subsidize the work despite this contribution, but the publishers were influenced by the consideration of their audience in the church. Part of the volume appeared from Herder Verlag in 1976 without Böll and without reference to the birthday under the title *Christentum innerhalb und ausserhalb der Kirche*

('Christianity Inside and Outside the Church'), edited by Elmar Klinger.

On Rahner's seventy-fifth birthday I edited a Festschrift for him which under the title *Wagnis Theologie* ('The Venture of Theology') brought together thirty-eight contributions from pupils and former collaborators of Rahner describing their experiences with his theology. This was published by Herder in 1979.

Elmar Klinger and Klaus Wittstadt organized a lengthy volume *Glaube im Prozess* ('Faith in Process') for Karl Rahner's eightieth birthday. It is devoted to Vatican II and various contributions stress Rahner's involvement in the Council. In addition it has an air of reconciliation about it, since it also contains articles by theologians who were not sympathetic to Karl Rahner's theology.

These four volumes which have been dedicated to Karl Rahner since 1964 are of interest to those who want to become more closely acquainted with his theology. For they contain lists of all his publications, and of articles and books which have been written by others about him, including critical ones.

However, mention must also be made of two foreign Festschrifts for Karl Rahner, *Teología y mundo contemporáneo*, ed. A.Vargas-Machuca, Madrid 1975, and *Theology and Discovery*, ed.W.J.Kelly, Milwaukee 1980. They bear witness to the international influence of Karl Rahner.

From Munich to Münster

The nomination of Rahner to the chair in Munich dates from 5 March 1964. He began lecturing in May of that year. Rahner thought extraordinarily highly of the personality and life-work of Romano Guardini generally.[115] He always counted Guardini as one of the great renewers of theology in the twentieth century. He was less attracted to Guardini's lecturing style, which seemed to him too esoteric, too aesthetic, too imprecise. He did not want to be, nor could he be, Guardini's successor in this sense. He dictated his lectures in advance and because of his concern for exactitude in wording did not lecture ex tempore. Guardini had been very much preoccupied with interpretations of poetry and other themes which attracted a wide educated public. Rahner spoke on the one theme which more than any other was close to his heart after his departure from Innsbruck, the concept of

Christianity. These Munich lectures, which later, after a great deal of revision, grew into the *Grundkurs des Glaubens* (*Foundations of Christian Doctrine*), were not a success in terms of the size of the audience. Rahner was regarded as too difficult, too demanding, not topical enough, too abstract. Other lectures which he gave in Munich simply arose out of his work at the Council: for two semesters he lectured on world and church after the Second Vatican Council – not a particularly original theme.

Moreover there was much that stood in the way of Rahner's spontaneity at that time. He felt overtaxed by the Council, he had exhausted himself by lecture commitments at home and abroad, he had taken on much too difficult publications which he had to supervise, and could not be surprised that the publishers pressed him to keep the agreed deadlines. 'They're quite right, too: publishing is a systematic matter,' he wrote to me from Munich on 13 January 1966. He was soon resigned as far as his hope for selfless collaborators was concerned: 'We must work with the people there are and not with those there should be,' he wrote to me on 13 April 1965.

In this situation, in North Germany he met Bernhard Kötting of the Theological Faculty of the University of Münster. Kötting again pressed him, as he had years earlier, to come to Münster. Rahner retorted that he regarded the obstacles in Rome – with the General – and in Munich, where the Jesuits were dependent on his income, as insuperable. But then he wrote to me: 'Afterwards it occurred to me that Münster could be attractive if in the next few years it were possible to begin a thorough reform of theological study with the people there along the lines of my ideas. Otherwise Münster no longer attracts me.' He mentioned various possibilities which he would realize with Metz and me, and thought: 'I now feel that there would be some opportunity for reform there and that could perhaps even dissuade Rome from a No.' And then he expressed the understandable wish: '*If* I went from here (?), of course I would like to avoid the impression that I was going because I had not succeeded. From that point of view the plan for reform would have to be coupled in some way with such a call' (Letter from Munich, 14 January 1966).

The Munich theological faculty helped him to decide to leave Munich. He wanted to be able to help graduates to qualify in theology – and not just in philosophy; he was and remained a theologian, and quite a few came to him in Munich because of his theology. Rahner's wish was not particularly ambitious: the kind of inter-faculty collaboration which he sought was also practised elsewhere. However, the Munich theological faculty refused him. Rahner declared, to Guardini's great disappointment, that he would leave Munich.[116]

When the call from Münster reached him, during the time when J.B.Metz was dean, he accepted. On 1 April 1947 he was nominated Ordinarius Professor of Dogmatics and the History of Dogma at the Catholic Theological Faculty of the University of Münster and moved from the Munich Jesuit house to the Marianum in Frauenstrasse, Münster.

For Rahner, Münster marked the beginning of a generally positive time. He lectured on grace, on Mary, on the doctrine of creation, christology and ecclesiology and for two semesters once again on the concept of Christianity. He gave seminars in dialogue form, also with J.B.Metz. This was the period of student unrest (1968). Rahner was impressed by the aims of this movement. He understood the young people and did not refuse to talk to them.

However, his physical strength was declining. He retired on 3 September 1971 and moved to the place where he had often lived during the holidays from Münster, the Jesuit writers' house in Munich.

'Official theologian' with Paul VI and Döpfner

The respect which even people who had earlier been somewhat restrained towards Rahner's theology showed him in the period immediately after the Council was expressed in numerous requests from official bodies for his collaboration. Here I can mention only a few striking episodes from this activity of Rahner's.

In 1966 he took an active part in an international theological conference in Nemi in Italy, at which he was deeply concerned that the church's doctrinal authorities should not condemn more recent attempts to see the limitations of the doctrine of original sin. He himself had radically changed his view over monogenism, human descent from just one couple, and the 'inheritance' from this of a primal guilt, for which he had still argued in Vol.VII of *LTK* (1963): he was ready and able to learn from the accounts of biblical scholars, natural scientists and friends like P. Schoonenberg.

In 1967, after contacts with German bishops, he wrote a long article in which he emphatically defended celibacy. The bishops had been panicked by the large number of priests and members of Orders who wanted to get married. Rahner did not do them this service simply on tactical grounds or out of a desire to support them. He regarded the concern for bourgeois marriage to be a *possible* expression of that *petit-bourgeois* life-style which he despised. In an interview he said,

> Just read Kierkegaard or other thinkers and then ask again whether – quite apart from the personal, individual destiny of the individual – there is not a bourgeois tendency behind the overall trend against celibacy even among our clergy in central Europe today. Today the mark of a Christian or a representative of Christianity is not renunciation of marriage but something that any 'reasonable' man of this life regards as crazy or nonsensical. And where we no longer produce this folly of the cross we are a socially animated bourgeoisie, content with the world, like the freemasons or other such people. Of course it cannot now be demonstrated deductively that this folly of the cross has to be proved by celibacy. Today one might even ask whether celibacy is its appropriate specific expression. But I would say that people who are against celibacy should at least be those who – to put things somewhat solemnly – volunteer for pastoral work among or care of lepers, who as worker priests live like simple workers. In that case all these tendencies would seem to me to be credibly Christian. But if they come from well-placed student counsellors or university professors with villas, I would say, 'In the end of the day, isn't this just a way of rounding off your bourgeois life-style?'[117]

One can see from this text that Rahner did not regard celibacy as intrinsically valuable. Apart from the fact that he found assent to his text on celibacy from people whose assent he suspected, he was later unhappy about arguments in which celibacy was made one of the supreme values, so that increasingly he spoke out in favour of voluntary celibacy.

When in 1967 the German bishops wrote a doctrinal letter to all who were entrusted by the church with the proclamation of faith, Rahner helped to compose it. It was concerned with a theological problem which had affected Rahner himself in earlier years: how 'binding' is the doctrine of the church as long as this doctrine is not yet provided with the protection of being an irrevocable dogma? For example, how binding is the doctrine in a papal encyclical as long as it does not contain a dogmatic definition? Rahner stressed the possibility of reforming such church doctrine and the freedom of conscience of the Christians involved as long as it was validated by loyalty to the church. A year later Rahner had occasion to quote his own text as that of the German bishops in connection with the encyclical *Humanae vitae*, which he regarded as capable of reform and indeed needing reform.[118]

In a process which the Roman Congregation of Faith under Cardinal Šeper sought to bring against Rahner's Flemish Dominican friend E.Schillebeeckx, in October 1968, Rahner was able to speak in Rome as *relator*, i.e. as it were as defender in Rome before the authorities. The process was rejected.

When Paul VI founded the International Theological Commission, Karl Rahner was immediately nominated a member (27 April 1969). At the first meeting of this papal commission on 6 October 1969 he gave the programmatic speech on significant contemporary theological questions. In the next year he addressed this commission on the theology of revolution (10 October 1970). Before his period of office ran out in 1974, however, he resigned from the commission, not only because it seemed to him to be too 'boring' and 'inefficient',[119] but also because he found his younger colleagues there malicious and arrogant. The climate was no longer what it had been at the Council.

He also belonged for some years to the faith commission of the West German bishops' conference. His attitude towards Küng was publicly known and much criticized: he would never have supported the withdrawal of the church's permission for him to teach. His support of papal infallibility derived directly from his as it were innate churchliness: he thought that he could detect in Küng's questioning the mentality of liberal Protestantism.[120] On the other hand he expressly defended the way in which Küng wrote about Jesus, without *a priori* repeating the formulae of faith. Only through the publication of his opinion in *Schriften* Vol.III was a further activity of Rahner within this faith commission made known: in 1976 he defended the scholarly position of the NT scholar Rudolf Pesch in respect of the 'brothers' of Jesus, which the bishops saw as a threat to the dogma of the virgin birth.

Between 1970 and 1975 he took part in the work of the joint synod of the West German dioceses. He was chosen to advise the German heads of Orders at the synod. It was in connection with this Würzburg synod that he wrote his controversial booklet *Strukturwandel der Kirche als Aufgabe und Chance* ('Changes in the Structure of the Church as a Task and an Opportunity', 1972). In it he raised three questions. Where do we stand? What should we do? How do we conceive of a church of the future? There is hardly any trace of it in the resolutions and the effect of this synod. During his activity in the synod – where for the last time the mutual sympathy of Cardinal Döpfner and Rahner was at work, he was a member of the special commission I, which had to present to the synod the basic document worked out by J.B.Metz under the title 'Our Hope'. Rahner identified himself fully with this document and defended it as far as he was able. His two public controversies with Cardinal Höffner of Cologne in 1971 over the divinity of Jesus and the indissolubility of marriage also became known in connection with the synod.

These episodes show that Karl Rahner had now become a kind of authority even for those holding office in the church.

International reputation

I once noted the languages other than the often-mentioned European languages into which Rahner's articles have been translated. The list is astonishing: Greek, Portuguese, Polish, Czech, Slovak, Hungarian, Swedish, Danish, Croatian, Catalan, Korean, Japanese, Indonesian and Vietnamese translations have been made, and a translation of *Foundations* into Kisuaheli is in progress. However, all that does not say anything about the reception of Rahner's theology abroad.

First of all, it must be said that in foreign countries, as in the German-speaking world, central statements of Rahner's became so established among interested Christians that many people did not realize how much in them they owed to Rahner. That there is more talk of uncreated grace which is God himself in his communication of himself than of created grace; that the universal will of God for salvation is taken with radical seriousness and that therefore children, pagans, atheists and others who die unbaptized are no longer thought to be destined to eternal punishment; that nature and grace are no longer torn apart and thought of in a two-storey scheme; that sacraments can be understood as realizations, actualizations of the church in particular central events of Christian existence: such views and similar ones which go back to Rahner are so widespread today that one can perhaps even speak of growing assent to him.

Otherwise it is impossible to establish a particular influence of Rahner in individual regions. For example, in France his suggestions for pastoral theology were enthusiastically taken up at the time of the Council, but people found his transcendental theological thought less accessible. In the USA a generation of Rahner's Jesuit pupils represents a broad middle position between wild progressives and reactionaries: Harvey Egan, Avery Dulles, Leo O'Donovan, Willliam V.Dych, David J.Roy, Donald Reck and others. In America there are Rahner lectures in colleges and a Rahner day; in one church there is a painted window which shows Rahner as a teacher of the church. From a distance it is impossible to tell how far his thought is influential. Rahner has many friends among the bishops and theologians of Latin America who are very important for Christianity there. Many in Spain are loyal to him, and these are not just Jesuits. He found a late 'group of sympathizers' at the Hungarian bishops' conference who often invited him as their guest in the last years of his life. This amazingly wide influence of an individual theologian, at least in terms of reputation, could not be explained without the journeys which he undertook untiringly and always cheerfully. Here it is impossible to give more than a few examples. Rahner often visited North America for lectures and talks. In Italy in 1966 he made an audacious and not very successful attempt to give lectures in Italian: in Turin, Genoa, Milan, Rome and Naples. In March and April 1968, at the invitation of the Protestant theological faculties he gave lectures in Scandinavia, in Copenhagen, Lund, Oslo, Uppsala, Helsinki and Abo Turku. In 1969 he spoke in Prague and Budapest, and in 1970 he travelled in Poland. He often went to Spain, among other things to a public discussion with J.B.Metz and J.Moltmann in Madrid in 1974. In October 1975 and 1980 he lectured to the Papal Urbaniana University in Rome which is specially concerned with missionary questions. A few weeks before his death he spoke in England and Hungary.

12 Dialogue

'Dialogue' and 'openness of the church to the world' arose as slogans at the time of Vatican II. Often there was not even a well-thought-out purpose behind them; often they were simply propaganda. Rahner was in dead earnest about dialogue. He was also quite unable to make even the smallest concession over anything in Christianity that he understood to be right or felt to be a real claim on the conscience. But he was convinced that truth and morality are also to be found outside the church and Christianity and that both Christianity and the church can learn from those outside. He was further convinced that Christianity and the church are still far from having found a language in which they could really communicate their message. He was ready to note language not shaped by faith and also to make himself understood with it.

Dialogue with natural scientists

In this spirit Rahner carried on a dialogue with representatives of the natural sciences. He was concerned to demolish the traditional prejudices of scientists against faith and the church, but he also untiringly called on them not to overestimate the range and methods of their sciences. In conversation with people like Konrad Lorenz he attempted to show that in human beings there is not just so-called evil, value-free aggression, but responsibility and guilt. He appealed to their consciences not to encourage developments the outcome of which could not be seen, like genetic engineering. But he learned from them to think in a rationally limited way in evolutionary terms. He learned to understand the history of God with the world and humanity as an evolutionary process which moves forward in qualitative 'leaps': from the inorganic to life, from the vegetative to consciousness, from the animal kingdom to the human world, from parents to the child, from humanity to God in man, in Jesus of Nazareth, from death to consummation. He termed these 'leaps' or transitions self-transcendence, and in so doing preserved the honour of humanity, including the honour of the natural sciences, and the honour of God: God alone can enable the finite to bring forth something really new. The old cannot ever really declare itself to be really new. But God enables the old to bring forth really new things so that the new in all truth emerges from the old. God and the natural forces do not compete with each other. The new, for example the child, is utterly from God and utterly, body and soul, from its parents.

Over against purely scientific thought or, even more generally, a positivistic view of the world which seeks to prohibit speaking about that which one cannot investigate and prove by the methods of the natural sciences, Rahner defended the right of theology to join in the conversation and therefore its right to have a place in the university. He emphatically pointed out that a natural scientist cannot speak scientifically about the nature of his discipline, about the meaningfulness of doing science. As soon as anyone begins to reflect on everything, away from individual matters – his research or his everyday life - he thinks and speaks philosophically and theologically, whether or not he is aware of the fact. Rahner saw it as the task of linguistic philosophy to demonstrate that theological statements are meaningful. He rejected the view that this demonstration, this verification, could only be provided by Christian praxis:

> There are very many other possibilities of overcoming modern positivism in principle and developing a method of verification of theology which on the one hand works with the conceptions and language of this modern Anglo-Saxon epistemology and on the other hand nevertheless attempts to demonstrate the justification of theology. My pupils in Münster, Helmut Peukert and Kuno Füssel, for example, have attempted such things.[121]

Dialogue with Marxists

The Paulusgesellschaft, in the framework of which Rahner primarily carried on his dialogue – as in the Institute of the Görresgesellschaft which I mentioned earlier – also offered him the opportunity of entering into the dialogue between Christianity and Marxism. Karl Rahner had no anxiety about contact with Marxists and Communists in the flesh. He openly called them 'my friends'. He had civic courage. Personal esteem bound him to people like Ernst Bloch, Milan Machovec, Roger Garaudy and some members of the Italian Communist party.

He was familiar with the Marxist accusations against bourgeois religion: he shared them. As a result of conversations with people from all over the world and from all levels of society he was also convinced that religion had been misused – and not only in the nineteenth century – as consolation with the beyond and that the masters and exploiters of all times had backed up their systems with appeals to a divinely willed eternal ordinance. He had great respect for the ethical impulses towards a humanizing change of the world which are contained in Marxism. But without false diplomacy he indicated the weak points and the inhumanities in Marxism by stressing that it is unacceptable for a Christian to sacrifice people of the present generation on the altar of Moloch's future in favour of a happier generation to come, and equally unacceptable to reduce humanity just to a bundle of chemical processes influenced by society.

In conversation with Marxists Rahner developed his important distinction between absolute future and future within the world.[122] He said that Christianity has no recipes for shaping the future within the world and that it therefore can and must associate itself with any real humanism so that the future within the world may become worthy of humanity. He said that it was the task of Christianity to show humanity as being on the way to an absolute future, to a future which cannot be planned and cannot be made, but comes of itself and consummates all things – humanity, history and the world: the absolute future which is only another name for God. But he had learned from Marxists that there must be a connection between the two futures, without Christianity being mere consolation with the beyond. Therefore Rahner emphatically said that a man misses his absolute future – God – if he does not work with all his power for the human realization of the future within the world. Rahner never naively assumed that people can realize the kingdom of God on this earth. He knew that the kingdom of God is promised to all men, living and dead, and that therefore the kingdom of God cannot by-pass the dead.

The kingdom of God presupposes the transformation of all that exists. But he was equally convinced that no one can enter the kingdom of God who does not make his own contribution towards changing existing circumstances in the direction of the divine promises, of freedom, justice and peace.

Here he saw an unsparing analysis of the present situation as an indispensable task. He found that the analysis of the situation in Latin America made by the Marxists is correct: the sub-continent is in deliberate and planned dependence, with all the consequences among wide areas of the population – lack of freedom and deprivation – which are also religious consequences: that people to whom Christian people do such things cannot believe the Gospel. Here he was not taken in by Marxists, but learned the situation through numerous conversations with those directly involved. He supported without reservation the view of the 1974 General Assembly of the Jesuits and of General Arrupe that the church in Latin America, the Philippines and elsewhere has to work for the *integral* liberation of people and that therefore the church may never be limited to a supposedly purely religious sphere because that would be acceptance and stabilization of injustice. He therefore showed solidarity with the theology of liberation, though he sometimes found that its practical zeal needed to be based on deeper theoretical reflection. When he was already fatally ill he supported the theologian Gustavo Gutierrez, whose existence in the church and therefore whose physical existence was threatened, in a letter to the bishops of Peru.

Karl Rahner was never one of those theologians who is enthusi-astic about progress. Characteristic of the way in which he evaluated the triumph of technology is the opinion which he gave at the request of Dutch television at the time of the first manned landing on the moon in 1969:

I will not belittle this gigantic effort and this triumph of the human domination of the world. I will not say that it should not have happened. But if some already set out to leave this our old earth, the others, the majority, who remain here should feel even more urgently the responsibility to work with just as much boldness and persistence, with just as many heroic renunciations, to make this old earth freer from war, hunger, misery and crass injustice. Otherwise this day would be an accusation: your intelligence has found the way to the distant moon, but your heart does not know the way to the misery of your brother who is near.[123]

Karl Rahner also took an active part in the institutionalized forms of dialogue. Like Metz and myself he was one of the first group of experts in the Vatican Secretariat for Non-believers, which was directed until 1980 by Cardinal König and had its heyday in the 1960s. The conferences of this secretariat first of all spoke *about* contemporary unbelief in the view of various sciences; the secretariat did not arrive at a real dialogue with non-believers. Therefore in 1967 Cardinal König suggested the foundation of an international dialogue journal which was to be shaped equally by Christians and atheists. The publisher Dr T.Herder-Dornreich offered König his good offices to bring this about; he asked me to help with the founding. On the side of the non-believers it was easy to find collaborators among the bourgeois Western humanists who had announced that they were atheists. The organization of the collaboration of Marxist atheists was difficult, since here the question of party allegiance and consideration of Eastern European countries played a large part. In a long conversation in December 1967, Cardinal König, the publisher Dr Hermann Herder and I failed to gain Roger Garaudy, at that time in the French Communist party, as an effective collaborator. So it was resolved that Rahner and I should edit the international journal *Dialog*. It appeared from 1968 up to and including 1974.

The collaboration of non-Christians and Christians in a council of fifty functioned admirably: the Protestant theologian and literary scholar Olaf Schmalstieg also succeeded in securing interesting contributions from the literary sphere, peace studies, and so on. But the welcome in the milieux for which the journal was intended was not friendly. Various people and organs with right-wing tendencies vigorously attacked the journal and also Rahner by name because of the unhampered minority of Communists. In a doctoral work for a leading Catholic layman and political scientist Rahner was accused of betraying the truth. On a visit which Rahner and I paid to Cardinal Döpfner in September 1969 to further the journal, Döpfner seemed tired and resigned. He saw himself exposed to constant attacks from the Catholic traditionalist circles in West Germany, while at the same time he had fallen into disrepute in the Vatican because in a request that a certain priest should be nominated suffragan bishop he had not notified Rome that the man had been involved in partisan battles during the war. The impression given by the Council that clergy and laity in the church had been embraced by a stream of warmth, love and openness began to disappear. It seemed that the idea of dialogue was also dead at the level of official individuals and groups, even before it had properly come alive. When even the publisher resigned, we ended work with the journal. Rahner later also regarded this initiative, too, as meaningful.[124]

Until the end of his life he did not give up hope of conversing with 'official' Marxist party members. He sought understanding in the interest of a peaceful future for the world and in the interest of the Christians of Eastern Europe. Shortly before his death, at the end of February and the beginning of March 1984, he had his last dialogue with Marxists. And this time he was invited by official party circles, by the Academy of Sciences in Budapest.

Protests

The comment about Cardinal Döpfner's mood in 1969 was already an indication of a change in the climate within the church in West Germany. The mood of a new start, dialogue and the 'opening of the church to the world' lasted for only a short time. Events in the secular world contributed to this: Catholicism in West Germany, which had hardly welcomed the Council and what it said about the church in the modern world, experienced the student unrest after 1968 and the change of government in 1969 as cruel blows of fate. It began the march into the ghetto. It began a process which can also be personalized and which can be noted internationally with the deaths of Cardinal Döpfner, Pope Paul VI and Cardinal Šeper. Rahner did not just oppose this situation by pointing untiringly to the tasks of the church and theology in the future. He also mentioned in specific protests signs of a way which in his view was quite disastrous. If we look at the main lines of Rahner's protests,[125] we can see that he opposed the shaping of the church by the personal religious, theological and political views of a few people; he defended the democratization of the church, wherever dialogue did not destroy an essential order which had grown up legitimately. He sought to keep as many people as possible in the church, and not to drive them out of Christianity into purely secular and political humanisms; he regarded talk of the 'slimming down' of congregations, Orders and so on as deeply un-Christian. Some examples of his protests should suffice.

In 1967 he used the occasion of a scandal in the so-called central committee of German Catholics to raise in public the apparently naive question, 'Who does this committee really represent?' He called for the representation of German Catholicism by free elections. In this connection he again put his demands for free speech and open dialogue in the church, and he called the unrest which arose from this inevitable and healthy.

He called the closure of the weekly magazine *Publik* in November 1971, allegedly for financial reasons (it was succeeded by the *Rheinischer Merkur*, which even now has to be subsidized to the tune of many millions of marks), a misfortune, a sign of poverty and a scandal for the West German church. He wrote his own preface to the first number of the free sequel to this magazine, *Publik-Forum*, in January 1972 and declared in it that *Publik* had died of the average mentality of the Catholic milieu in West Germany and the consequence could only be that the milieu must be changed.

In 1973 he and Metz together argued for the preservation and encouragement of the former student communities, which offered room for free initiatives, were notably characterized by student involvement, and also sought to offer a home to students who could not totally identify themselves with the church. The opposing memorandum by J.Ratzinger, which stressed the sacramental character of 'community' and declared that the central spiritual task of the community could not be synodalized, thus rejecting 'basic communities', won through.

In November 1977, along with other theologians, Rahner signed a memorandum against making the distribution of church aid in Latin America dependent on the political behaviour and tranquillity of the recipients. Rahner had been convinced by Jesuits who were active locally of the rightness of the criticisms.

In autumn 1979 Rahner protested publicly against the fact that, following an intervention by Cardinal Ratzinger, which was not provided for by the law, Herr Maier, the Minister for Cult in

Bavaria, did not recognize J.B.Metz, who was top of the list, as the successor to Heinrich Fries in Munich and thus indicated that the two representatives of Catholicism in West Germany did not recognize the justification and freedom of a political theology.

In winter 1981 Rahner took part in public and direct protests against the dismissal from office of the Jesuit General Pedro Arrupe, who was seriously ill.

In 1982 he appealed to the political world to take steps towards unilateral disarmament and to put a radical end to the arms race. He based his appeal on the Sermon on the Mount and thus identified himself with those who see specific rules for conduct there. As we can see in Vol.XVI of his *Schriften*, he required people to recognize a Christian morality more by condemning a rearmament which is becoming nonsensical than by condemning the pill.

These protests, to which a whole series of less well-known initiatives by Rahner could be added, were all unsuccessful.In the last year of his life Rahner coined the phrase 'the winter time', of the period in which the church had already begun to live. This saying, too, indicated the sometimes almost incomprehensible hope of Rahner that the winter – however long the frosty and troubled time might be – would be followed by a spring.

Ecumenical dialogue

From the beginning, Karl Rahner's theology sought an ecumenical dialogue. One can continually find in him an effort to learn from Protestant theology, to extend the horizon of his own questions by the problems it raises and, without succumbing to false compromises, to formulate his own theology and the dogma of the church in such a way that they no longer present difficulties to Protestant Christians and theologians, other than those that are inevitable. Some of what Rahner has said about justification, 'righteous yet a sinner', transubstantiation in the eucharist, the concept of *opus operatum*, personal attitudes and faith in connection with the sacraments, and divorce, can only be evaluated completely from this perspective. Here again and again we find the following basic consideration on the part of Rahner: one may never regard even a dogmatically binding and permanently valid formulation only as the unsurpassable end of a process which has now been concluded. It must also be regarded as a formulation which – regardless of its permanent validity – is open to the mystery, which never says all that it is true and important for Christians, which can provoke real difficulties in understanding among non-Catholics and therefore is the abiding task of Catholic theology which always has to be fulfilled.

Rahner's ecumenical work was done in the awareness that Catholic theology must always also look within for 'guilt', i.e. the cause of the opposition of other Christians to the theology of its church, because even his Catholic theology remains the theology of a searching and fallible human being.

If we attempt to see what in Rahner's own theology corresponds to Protestant theology, then we can find it primarily in the sphere of the common legacy from Paul and Augustine of the primacy of divine grace which brings about the will, the ability and the *de facto* performance of all that is good, so that a person has nothing of himself on which he can take a stand as an autonomous contribution before God. With the Reformers, Rahner could say *sola gratia*, through grace alone. There is a parallel between his theology of the word and the high estimation of the Word of God among Protestant Christians. He even understands a sacrament as a particularly tangible, concentrated form of the word and sees the word in the sacrament as having decisive importance, whereas the material elements only serve to clarify the word. For Rahner, Holy Scripture contains all that God has revealed for our salvation; in this sense it is enough as a source of faith, so that Rahner can also say with the Reformers, *sola scriptura*, scripture alone suffices.

However, there are also basic Protestant positions which Rahner could not share and to which he was even honestly opposed. These include a view of grace in which God gives grace to the sinner only as it were from outside like a lord of the manor. For Rahner, grace is the communication of God himself which transforms people inwardly, which brings it about that a person does not continually sin. So he also rescues human honour before God. In Rahner, the biblical theme of the wrath of God, which plays only a minor role in the New Testament, has completely fallen into the background. The God who gives himself in love regardless of consequences, whom Rahner experiences, no longer has any trace of anger in him. Therefore the theologies of sin, judgment and the cross are no longer of primary importance for him. Since Rahner wanted to be a theologian who saw church theology as not being dependent on the discoveries of biblical criticism, as I have already pointed out, a kind of Protestant way of doing biblicistic theology through abundant references to words in the Bible was always alien to him.

I have already mentioned earlier the outward mark of Karl Rahner's entry into ecumenical conversations. At the beginning of his activity he was more in contact with Protestant theologians who were particularly open to the Catholic church, like Hans Asmussen and Max Lackmann. In April 1961 we were together in Taizé, and from then on his relationship with the Christians there was never broken. He carried on profound philosophical conversations with Heinrich Ott. He carried on a correspondence with Karl Barth and Rudolf Bultmann. There were dialogues with Wolfhart Pannenberg, Eberhard Jüngel and Oscar Cullmann, and with the theologians of the World Council, above all Lukas Vischer. He appeared on the platform with Jürgen Moltmann, Ernst Fuchs and Gerhard Ebeling.

He tried to involve his church in active ecumenism, but in vain. No notice was taken of his book about possible agreements in questions of ministry. The book he wrote with Heinrich Fries in 1983 on the union of the churches took the demands of the church as an institution with the most radical seriousness. The prior condition for the union of institutions is not the resolution of problems in the sphere of controversial theology; the churches have here and now, in a critical situation for Christianity, a duty to bring about their institutional unity and then expect that full unity in faith and theology will emerge from this union.[126]

Karl Rahner also joined in dialogue with the Jews. In the 1960s he carried on conversations with E.L.Ehrlich and F.G.Friedmann, and his 1982 dialogue with Pinchas Lapide over what Jews and Christians have in common and what fundamental differences there are between them has been published.[127] In the last years of his life, as the last volumes of his *Schriften* show, he paid increasing attention to Islam. One important theme of Rahner's theology, his view of the Trinity, could be as pioneering in the dialogue with Islam as his 'christology from below'.

13   Criticism of Karl Rahner

Naturally Karl Rahner's theology, like any theology, is the work of a fallible and inadequate human being; and because of its extent, it is certainly very open to attack. Even this short book in no way attempts to present Rahner's views as being above all criticism. There is a criticism of Rahner which takes place in the sphere of strict academic discussion. Of course Rahner sometimes has weak spots at which his views need supplementing or correction. For example, he carried on his discussion with the Jew Pinchas Lapide as an individual, in the light of the theology of Rahner, and not in the context of the Jewish-Christian conversation, which in the meantime had moved on further. That indicates that although he was asked about almost everything by outsiders, he was not up to date with all developments to the same degree. The bibliographies indicate such criticisms of Rahner in the specialist literature; it is not possible here to go further into those involved and their arguments. However, there are forms of criticism of Rahner which are not so much on points of detail as on matters of principle. Mention must be made of them in an introduction to Rahner's life and work.

Criticism from the 'right'

If we leave the earlier objections from Rome on one side, since these have been discussed at length, there is a criticism of Rahner from the 'right'. It was expressed from Vatican II on, and comes from groups of Catholic traditionalists. Instead of many quotations from brochures and pamphlets, the voice of the former Mainz church lawyer Georg May may speak for all:

The victorious course of Rahner's theology could not be explained had its author not succeeded in making some extremely influential, but insufficiently theologically informed members of the hierarchy, first and foremost from German-speaking countries, completely dependent on his ideas. What was offered by Rahner has been taken up above all by Döpfner, presented by him to the German bishops' conference and accepted by them. Rahner has given the German bishops, especially the president of the German bishops' conference, the theses which they imposed on the Council and pressed on the Apostolic See; Rahner's theology became dominant at the Second Vatican Council...

We can see from Rahner's theology what a calamity is evoked when the fate of the church and the faith (as far as it is in human hands) is handed over to theologians. Rahner's theology is also an example of the way in which a theologian is driven further down a slippery slope: a theology which serves each everyday need, which justifies everything and excuses what should properly be called guilt and stubbornness, becomes an ideology. It ought to be equally clear that such a theology digs its own grave; as a result of the relative slowness with which sociological and legal positions change, and thanks to the moral excuse that it gives to a morbid society in the face of the radical demand of God, it may still be tolerated in certain positions for a while, but in the end it will be swept away as being quite superflous. It is a theology which fits in with the twilight of German Catholicism. Rahner has served his Munich sponsors faithfully; but he is now in ruins along with the whole fiasco of the 'reforms' that he shaped and introduced. With his theology Rahner sought to build up the church; he has contributed towards knocking it down.[128]

It is clear that there can be no discussion with such a view; it is either right or wrong, and incapable of dialogue. Rahner had to experience the way in which bishops were made to feel insecure by complaints, insults, rumours and so on of the kind fabricated and circulated in a Catholic sub-culture (a small minority), to abandon the way of renewal and openness, and thus also to give up 'missionary' recruitment for the church. Criticism and its consequences affected him deeply, all the more since he knew with every fibre of his heart how false they were. They brought Cardinal Döpfner prematurely to the grave.

Criticism from the 'liberals'

Some of Rahner's critics found his way of seeking the 'nucleus' of a dogmatic statement, of stressing an underlying intention which was valid for today, to be both roundabout and dishonest. They did not see anything terrifying in the assumption that the church made dogmatic formulations as a result of wrong ideas or for political considerations. They regarded it as a demand of the hour that the church should recognize that at all times it was guilty and subject to error, and thus in all solidarity with sinners and those who had gone astray. They therefore felt it superfluous to look for an abiding nucleus, still significant today, in dogmatic statements which simply seem scandalous to the majority of intellectuals. Rahner tried to explain what led him to his roundabout approach and the way in which he thought. He asked what reason an inquirer could have at all for trusting the message of his own church if the church itself *a priori* doubted the basic grounds for the truth of this message. He asked what justification people of today have for supposing that there was error or an intent to deceive *in their own day* among earlier Christians of the church convinced that they were formulating their belief in true statements. And finally he asked whether in an institution moving from error to error it was still possible seriously to speak of a church which maintained its identity through history; and if this identity was lost, the church had also lost its beginning in Jesus.[129]

Criticism from the 'left'

Rahner was occasionally accused of having sought to safeguard the truth of theological statements by epistemological considerations instead of pointing to praxis as the only possibility of 'proving' God. So he remained an idealistic theoretician whose basic model was the relationship of God to the isolated human individual. You, we and history are blotted out of this model. Criticism of this kind was often expressed by earlier pupils of Rahner and Metz like Marcel Xhaufflaire, Johannes Caminada and others. It seems to me that they fail to recognize the content and consequences of Rahner's doctrine of the unity of divine love and human love.

Karl Rahner and Hans Urs von Balthasar

Hans Urs von Balthasar, born in 1905, a Jesuit until 1950 and since then a free-lance spiritual writer, director of his own publishing house and a secular institute, was at one time among the close friends of Karl Rahner. I have already described their joint deliberations in Munich. Direct contact between the two lasted until the beginning of the 1960s. When I was working on the Festschrift for Hugo Rahner (1961), Karl Rahner and I visited Hans Urs von Balthasar and Adrienne von Speyr in their house in the Münsterplatz in Basle. At this last meeting between the two theologians, the exchange of ideas was open and friendly. For a while afterwards von Balthasar sent his books to Rahner; in one he put the inscription 'Write a theology of the cross!' I do not know from what point the alienation can be dated precisely. It is certain that it did not begin from Rahner's side. He always regarded von Balthasar as one of the most significant theologians of the twentieth century. His own verdict was: 'Theologians like H.U.von Balthasar, in whom historical scholarship truly serves a living, ongoing theology which confronts the questions of today, are very rare in Germany – indeed perhaps he is unique.'[130] Personal factors contributed to the alienation. Von Balthasar was bitter because he was completely excluded from Vatican II, and in 1963 he was a rival of Rahner's for Romano Guardini's chair. But this does not explain everything. Since the Council and above all since von Balthasar's little book *Cordula oder der Ernstfall* (1966), for von Balthasar Rahner has been the great theological opponent who makes faith inadmissibly easy, who adapts to the needs of contemporaries, and trivializes the seriousness of God's history with humanity.

Von Balthasar experienced the deadly seriousness of the suffering of God above all from the visions of Adrienne von Speyr. From there he arrived at an inner view of the divine Trinity in which the drama of love was played out in the form of a deadly rivalry between Father and Son. Von Balthasar held that the only important task of the believer was to perceive this divine movement of love in humility and gratitude and to enter into the Son's way of obedience. He therefore directed Christians towards contemplation and strict asceticism. He expressly declared that that could not be thg way of the 'masses'. From antiquity to the present day the 'masses' in Christianity and the church had been problematical; they only made a fragmentary contribution which could not be considered further. Von Balthasar sought to compensate for the one-sidedness and élitism of this notion by his hope for universal reconciliation: as the Son of God has himself suffered all of hell, as he has suffered the punishment of the Father, it is to be hoped that the God who henceforth will not be angry will not abandon any of the 'masses'.

Rahner suffered very much under the attacks of Balthasar, especially as von Balthasar later also accused him of specifically heretical errors.[131] He asked from where von Balthasar had obtained his knowledge of the inner life of the deity. He was disturbed that von Balthasar *a priori* would not attempt to communicate what he had seen in visions to the people 'of today', while he himself in his fundamentally anti-élitist thought felt compelled to mediate: how can I bring Christianity today so near to people that it can really get to them? Here he was aware that those who are concerned to communicate to others are more open to attack than the one who declares *a priori*, 'Either you have this vision and insight or you don't.'

Once Rahner publicly defended himself by saying in an interview:

> If I wanted to counter-attack, I would say that there is a modern tendency (I will not say theory, but tendency) – in both Hans Urs von Balthasar and Adrienne von Speyr (of course far more in the latter), but also independently in Moltmann – to conceive of a theology of the death of God which seems to me to be basically gnostic. To use somewhat primitive terms, there is no point in my getting out of my muck and filth and despair if – to put it crudely – God is just as mucky. It is my consolation that God, if and in so far as he has entered this history as his own, has at least done so in a different way from me. For I am *a priori* cemented into this hideousness, whereas God – if this word is to have any meaning at all – is in a true and authentic and comforting sense the *Deus impassibilis*, the God who is incapable of suffering.[132]

Radically different experiences of God led to irreconcilable theological positions.

Karl Rahner and Johann Baptist Metz

The personal friendship of Karl Rahner with Johann Baptist Metz, which lasted from Metz's studies in Innsbruck in the 1950s until

Rahner's death, constantly emerged from the private sphere. Rahner spoke of 'my friend Metz', Metz dedicated various books to Rahner 'in deep bonds of friendship'. For Rahner, theological conversation with Metz was always helpful. In his early days Rahner had in fact formulated his philosophy of religion, the stages in the knowledge of God, 'objectively' in terms of a movement of the human spirit towards things, towards objects. Rahner owed his encounter with a philosophy and theology of intercommunication primarily to Metz. Rahner once said in the 1970s:

> Man experiences himself by experiencing the other *person* and not the other *thing*. Man could not achieve a self-withdrawal from a world consisting exclusively in material objects any more than he could from his own body, the concrete experience of which as it *de facto* exists also in fact presupposes an encounter with the physicality of other persons. Self-experience is achieved in the unity between it and the experiences of other persons. When the latter is harmoniously achieved, the former succeeds as well. He who fails to discover his neighbour has not truly achieved realization of himself either. He is not in any true sense a concrete subject capable of identifying himself with himself, but at most an abstract philosophical subject, and a man who has lost himself. The subject's experience of himself and of the Thou who encounters him, is one and the same experience under two different aspects, and that too not merely in its abstract formal nature, but in its concrete reality as well, in the degree of success or failure with which it is achieved, in its moral quality as an encounter with the real self and with one's fellow in love or hatred. Thus the concrete relationship of the subject to himself is inextricably dependent upon the factor of how a subject encounters his fellow man.[133]

Here the influence of Metz is clearly evident. It can also be found in Rahner's contributions on the relationship between philosophy and theology, the love of God and the love of man, the I-Thou relationship, and the theology of freedom (in *Schriften*, Vol.VI), in his remarks on political love and Christian humanism (in Vol.VIII); on the social function of the church and the future (in vol.IX); on the theology of revolution (in Vol.X); and on the theme of *memoria* (in Vol.XII). Though Rahner sometimes said that he did not know what was meant by the 'political theology' of his friend Metz, in reality he knew very well.

For example, he acknowledged his debt to Metz's view of discipleship of Jesus as follows:

> If Christianity is love of God and the neighbour, if love of God today can only be realized in a mysticism of the experience of the nearness of God, and if love of the neighbour can only be realized by perceiving a social and political task which everyone has, then what Metz says is, I think, clear: that Christianity, particularly today, has a mystical and a social component. I say 'particularly today', because without the mystical component a merely external indoctrination does not do justice to the existence of God and Christianity and its content. And I would say that precisely today, a social and political or a social element is particularly significant because the person of today will not find true love of neighbour which comes from God and bears witness to God credible if it is limited to an intimate sphere between human beings and does not perceive the real socio-political and socio-critical task.[134]

So it is all the more surprising that Metz criticized Rahner and his theology of transcendence.[135]

I once, to Rahner's satisfaction, challenged Metz,[136] because I found his comparison of Rahner with the hedgehog and his wife in the folk tale unfair, and because it seemed to me bad to accuse Rahner of 'conjuring tricks'. I had in mind the way Metz's comments were phrased; the actual content of what he was saying, though, put a serious question to Rahner and the whole theological tradition, which is important enough to be mentioned here, at least in broad outline.

Karl Rahner's experience of God did not exclude the fearful state of the world and what men do to one another. Rahner had contemporary experience of the human catastrophe which is referred to as 'Auschwitz' and took it into account in his theology, nor was he blind to the possibility of nuclear destruction. But he was capable of letting literally everything go over into his God.

A famous schema in his theology uses the terms 'transcendental' and 'categorial', and thus makes difficult reading for those without prior interest. The two terms can mean different things in Rahner. In the present context they mean that God loves humanity with an incomprehensible, effective love – the 'transcendental' aspect, for this love extends from God's eternity, through the coming into being of the world, the rise of humanity, the incarnation of God, all down history to the universal consummation in God. The love of God seeks to come to human beings, to enter into their consciousness and change them – the 'categorial' aspect. Here, in history, God creates instruments and symbols by means of which he seeks to support his advent, e.g. the church. But 'transcendentally' everything is predetermined for good, even if the vast majority of people reject or forget God, or if the church fails. God certainly wants human beings to assent to his salvation, but he also means them to be saved even without their assent (apart from the 'dark' case of the guilty repudiation of love when it is recognized). This is a God who loves 'unfathomably' beyond all human understanding.

This image of God – which arose out of an experience of God – certainly does not belittle human suffering. Rahner was aware of torture and despair. But he always pointed to what lay 'behind' and 'afterwards', and so it was that he sometimes talked about human life, its drama, history and tragedy, as though it were past. He often spoke of the conclusion of human history as the echoes of a clap of thunder in a departing storm, and in his farewell speech at Freiburg in 1984 he said of death:

> When the angels of death have carted away the useless rubbish that we call our history from the spheres of our spirit..., when all the stars of our ideals with which we have draped ourselves by appropriating the heaven of our existence, have faded and been quenched..., when our previous life, however long, seems to be just one short explosion of our freedom, which seemed to us extended, as in a time-retarder...[137]

It is important to take note of some other almost incomprehensibly optimistic remarks of Rahner about the specific suffering of humanity.

> The last and most real problem which is not taken account of is this absolute sovereignty of the infinite, incomprehensible God and with it the hope that against all the appearance of hideous humanity which seems to think of anything but God

and which in a fearful way even sins against itself, in the end happiness will win through.[138]

Or:

For me the history of humanity, despite all the disastrous things which have happened to men, even despite Auschwitz and all the catastrophes which perhaps we must still fear as a result of the exhaustion of natural resources and nuclear madness, is a history of salvation, a universal history of the power of grace and divine love, a history in which we can hope for *all human beings* and not just for a few.[139]

Or also:

I'm all for the courageous struggle for a better economy, for a better social future and I believe that the person who is really convinced of this must take responsibility for this social obligation before the judgment seat of God. When all is said and done, believers cannot and must not allow people who do not believe in this absolute future to get the better of them. I would say that if the world is destroyed by atomic weapons or slips further and further into economic misery, that would be all too horrible and frightful. And everyone is obliged before God's eternal judgment to do everything in his or her power to prevent such things from happening. One day we must give a reckoning for this. But if a people or humanity were to fall into the abyss, then I would still be firmly convinced – and I hope to keep this conviction – that even such an abyss always ultimately ends in the arms of an eternally good, eternally powerful God.[140]

For Rahner, neither individual nor collective death meant 'the end'.

The following remark shows how much this hope extending beyond history was bound up with Rahner's personal relationship with God:

It is not the future prospects which provide hope but the fact that despite all the external improbabilities, which are perhaps increasing, there are still people who believe in God as the absolute mystery of their existence with an ultimate seriousness, who do not evade unconditional responsibility in their lives, who pray, who accept death. And if there were no longer even anyone there, accursed and abandoned, I would make God the joy that I still have.[141]

For Johann Baptist Metz the question is whether this relationship to God does not at the same time turn its back on the suffering in the world which is invisible or is suppressed by force, the wordless suffering of the poor and the oppressed. He asks whether 'Auschwitz' must not go deeper into our relationship with God, whether in view of the catastrophes of humanity we should not ask more radically what 'meaning' can still be rescued after them, what kind of God, what kind of spirituality. Thus in an development in his thinking from about 1965 – in conversation with Ernst Bloch, Walter Benjamin, Jewish thought, Kierkegaard and Bonhoeffer – Metz arrives at 'his' theology which, while remaining true to Rahner's inspiration, nevertheless seeks to avoid the obvious danger of an attitude of apathy, a lack of sensibility to historical catastrophes. In contrast to Rahner, Metz is afraid of a complete questioning of the history of God with humankind. The 'apocalyptic goad' in the Jewish-Christian heritage, and in Jesus too, reminds him that humanity can lose God and that God's predilection for humanity can go wrong. This poses a question to Rahner, a question of deadly seriousness to Christian theology as a whole.

14 Concentration

In his old age Karl Rahner was very much concerned with the concentration of Christianity: how would it be possible to put into a very concentrated form what Christianity believes and seeks to practise, not because brevity is a virtue in itself but in order to remove the false impression that God has revealed an unconnected mixture of truths of faith in far distant times which have to be accepted without distinction if one is not to lose eternal salvation? In his attempt to express Christianity in a concentrated way, Rahner wanted to begin at the deepest dimension, the deepest desires of men and women, and formulate the answer in the most contemporary language possible, without repeating worn out, empty concepts. Thus he understood the human question to be:

> I need a final answer to the deepest mystery that I am to myself; I want to have a relationship with God; I want a last hope that my existence is finally worthwhile and ultimately true. I also want to feel in solidarity with the people of the past, who are not simply the presupposition of some kind of utopian future of happiness and a consumer society. Where is there an answer to all these questions, and a hundred like them, if not in Christianity? For the real message of Christianity consists in the answer to the questions I have indicated, in this one last hope.[142]

And this is just one attempt by Rahner to express in concentrated form what being a Christian means:

> Being a Christian means worshipping God, loving him, entrusting oneself to his incomprehensibility and the incomprehensibility of his dispensation, knowing that there is an eternal life which consists in the immediacy of the vision of God after death. All this relationship to God is supported and legitimated by Jesus Christ, because in view of him, his cross and resurrection, in view of the unity between God and man which is given unsurpassably through him, we can trust that by God's victorious grace, this task of our life to accept God himself in immediacy will really succeed. That these people who thus venture to be bold towards God because of Jesus Christ form a community of faith which is called church; that this community of faith has a history, a social structure which lays obligations on the individual, with all that the average Christian knows of his church – that is quite obvious. It is also obvious that the Christians and their church must intercede and work in the power of the Holy Spirit for justice, love and peace in a world which is treated as God's creation.[143]

From 1967 on, Karl Rahner made the proposal that 'short formulations' of Christian belief should be developed, and he made a number of attempts in this direction. These formulations were meant to demonstrate what are indispensable, indisposable, necessary elements of belief for the inquirer. In this process Rahner also attempted to listen to the people, namely to detect the *de facto* catechism by which believers live today and which is far from containing everything that is offically presented as the content of faith. The 'basic course in faith' which Rahner developed in many versions from 1964 onwards and had published in 1976 (*Grundkurs des Glaubens*; the English translation of 1978 was entitled *Foundations of Christian Faith*) represents an extended version of this process of concentration. In it he wanted to provide an introduction to the concept of Christianity in a series of reflections, to express the essentials of the Christian doctrine of faith at an attractive level, in a form which called for hard thinking, but did not make an excessive use of technical language. He himself set out his aims for the 'basic course' in Vol. XIV of his *Schriften* and there made it clear that he was aware that this 'basic course' was not immediately suitable for a wide circle of his readers but had to be 'translated' and 'popularized'. He included his short formulations in the volume. *Foundations of Christian Faith* is nothing like a *summa* of Rahner's theology, since he also spoke on numerous theological themes which do not appear in the book at all. Rather, in accordance with the doctrine of Vatican II, *Foundations* speaks of a hierarchy of truths of faith, the essential and indispensable side of Christian faith, and attempts to support it with theoretical arguments, i.e. to make it credible to thinking men and women.

In the last years of his life, Karl Rahner's thought about God concentrated increasingly on the incomprehensibility of God. Once – in 1967 – Rahner himself confessed that a remark by Hans Urs von Balthasar about Erich Przywara had terrified him. On Przywara von Balthasar said: 'He was probably the only one to have the language in which the word God can be heard without the levity and frivolity produced by the loud chatter of our average theology.'[144] In an article about the incomprehensibility of God dating from 1974, Rahner observed that the theme had preoccupied him intensively in recent times.[145] God as absolute mystery, God as complete incomprehensibility and yet the inescapable destiny of man: for Rahner that is not some part of the doctrine of God in which one property of God is expressed alongside others, but the centre and embodiment of all that a man and theologian can know of God and say of him. That radically changes the concept of revelation.

Revelation does not mean that the mystery is overcome by gnosis bestowed by God, even in the direct vision of God; on the contrary, it is the history of the deepening perception of God *as* the mystery. This continues in the direct presence of God afforded by what we call the beatific vision and can only be sustained in the loving surrender to the enduring mystery. It is the lost and not the blessed soul who perceives everything as infinite variety and so perceives nothing at all. The blessed abandons himself unconditionally to the direct self-communication of the mystery of the *deus absconditus* from which come love and salvation. If the theoretical intellect is understood as the capacity for conceptual mastery and comprehension, then beatitude means that the theoretical intellect is set free to love the mystery, which lays total hold on us by its direct presence. The history of revelation, then, consists in the growing awareness that we are involved with the permanent mystery and that our involvement becomes ever more intense and exclusive. If revelation is seen in this perspective, there is certainly a great deal more to say about it than we usually find in discussions about it. But if the climax of revelation, the communication of the Spirit of God himself, takes place when a man loses everything in death except God, and *in this way* achieves blessedness, then the history of revelation can well be written in the manner proposed here. In any history nothing can ultimately be explained without reference to the ending. In our case the ending is the advent of God who is the enduring mystery and is accepted in love. In that history, therefore, the mystery is not removed by a slow process of attrition; rather, all the provisional realities are dismantled which can lead to the belief that we can only achieve a relationship to God through what we believe we know about him.[146]

That is God; he is as real as love is real, and he has the basic property that love has – namely of being incomprehensible. Rahner never grew tired of praising *human love*, because as a miracle it points to the incomprehensibility of God:

But this nature of God's love, which is revealed particularly and ultimately only in the acceptance of his incomprehensibility as beatifying and not as annihilating, is also accessible to us in the light of lesser experiences that we have otherwise in personal love. At the point where one person encounters another in really personal love is there not an acceptance of what is not comprehended, an acceptance of what we have not ourselves perceived and consequently not mastered in the other person, the person who is loved? Is not personal love a trusting surrender without reassurance to the other person, precisely in so far as the latter is and remains free and incalculable?[147]

And in an article on 'The Inexhaustible Transcendence of God' we have this section based on his own experience:

If this is not to be selfishness in twos, love on the part of one must really be meant for the other, really for that person as such and in himself, and not for his importance to the one who loves him, not for the happiness he gives to the lover, not for the security he assures, but actually for himself, as he is meaningful, good and lovely for himself in his uniqueness, impregnability and unexploitability. That is not to say that it could not be expected, would not be hoped, that this other person, who is loved, would impart himself to someone who would respond to the love he received, would grant understanding, security and everything else that blooms in mutual love. But if in love the last resort and tacitly what is sought is one's own happiness and the loved one is not loved for his own sake, if that loved one's gratitude is not accepted by the other partner as a wholly gratuitous miracle but was the very thing sought tacitly and without admitting it by one's outgoing love, then this love has already lost its true nature and been turned into selfishness, no matter how gratifying it now seems to be. True love is self-abandoning, never returning to itself.[148]

15 The Last Years and Days

Karl Rahner had a good deal to do with death during his life. Like all men and women he experienced the death of relations. In his youth he had to part with friends. He lost fellow Jesuits in the war and through executions in the Nazi period. He was present at the death of his sixty-eight year old brother Hugo and his 101 year old mother. He spoke much of dying and death and wrote much about them. The many people who had direct contact with him, who loved him, will have asked how Rahner himself died. I am certain that it is utterly in keeping with his views to talk about that, since he wanted to speak publicly about all that was really important in his life: his experience of God, love, Jesus, and not to spread the cloak of bourgeois, polite discretion over them.

In 'retirement' in Munich, which for Rahner, like his previous life, was a state of restlessness, in addition to the usual lecturing and the indefatigable writing, he was also honorary Professor of Interdisciplinary Questions relating to Theology and Philosophy at the Jesuit High School for Philosophy there (until 1 October 1971). This High School was founded as the successor to the study centre at Pullach which was abandoned. Rahner occasionally lectured there and at the theological faculty in Innsbruck and took part in seminar exercises. As often as he could, he kept in contact with students. J.B.Metz and I repeatedly invited him as a guest to our students in Münster, and I think with gratitude of the epigram that he produced at his last colloquium with 'my' students: 'Knowing is the revenge of those who understand nothing.'

Circumstances for living and working in Munich were not very pleasant for the aged Rahner. He was increasingly attracted to the Jesuit house where he had had his most productive and dramatic time, in Innsbruck. He thought it important to move 'with the permission of the authorities'; in autumn 1981 that was granted. The Innsbruck Jesuits also provided him with fine rooms for a Rahner Archive, and in Frau Elfriede Oeggl he had a collaborator who conserved his strength and also drove the car which had become indispensable.

Since the end of the 1950s Rahner had often been seriously ill, but he had developed a technique of making himself fit for work again after long stays in hospital, so that such a stay was no longer anything out of the ordinary for his friends. He often also referred privately to the end of his life.

I would like to quote some examples from his letters to me, because they show how growing old and dying were present in his life in an undramatic and unsentimental way.

In May 1962, a month before the preliminary censorship, I had well-meaningly warned him against 'stirring up' the Romans. He replied to me on 19 May 1962; 'But look, what should I be afraid of? If I were condemned to the life of a Carthusian, then that

would really be all right by me. I would very much like to die in
possession of all my faculties, I think you can understand that.
And so that too is ultimately behind such a self-display.'

Pressed by work shortly before the Council he wrote: 'I'm
behind in everything. And that is my great grief. It's never been
like this before; I'm not only constantly under pressure and
overworked, but I can no longer meet my commitments properly.
And I don't know what will happen and what I should do. Oh,
Herbert, I'm growing old. That's natural, but wearisome and
painful' (24 September 1962).

On 2 March 1963 he wrote from Rome: 'So I shall soon be
sixty. Good God! We live to die. So we should not complain that
the dress-rehearsal of life is becoming increasingly demanding.'

In a letter of 21 May 1963 there is the admonition: 'The most
important thing: for the sake of God and all the saints look after
your health. It's fine to be dead. But not to be dying. So one should
live (live!) sufficiently long that one does not take long to die, like
Hürth, of whom his friend Tromp yesterday grimly said that one
cannot see in him any *desiderium naturale nec supernaturale
beatitudinis* (any natural or supernatural longing for bliss), who
cannot live and cannot die.'

I would like to quote one more fine and lengthy passage from
Rahner's letters to me. In summer 1982 I had asked him for a few
ideas for a doctoral student who wanted to work on a theology
of old age. On 16 July 1982 he replied:

Unfortunately I haven't many ideas to offer your doctoral
student. And what I have are rather muddled. Has she reflected
why Jesus could die so early and why we poor Christians must
do something that Jesus himself did not do? I'm not sure now
what I myself have written about old age, most recently in the
Festschrift for Dirks (I think). She should also see what forms
of behaviour are recommended in contemporary medical and
psychological gerontology, and ask whether there are corre-
sponding Christian virtues. What about age and death? Does
one suppress the thought of death more in old age than in
youth? Does everyone age in the same way? If not, as seems
likely, has that anything to do with the fact that our life is not
under our control? Is the saving acceptance of death really the
acceptance of old age, because nothing else can be done in

death? Some years ago I wrote a piece about the stages towards Christian consummation (or something of the sort). Are these stages not much more connected with the biological and psychological development towards old age than the adepts in ascetism think (*consummatus in brevi, explevit multa tempora*; the saints who die young are praised in some such terms as this). Is not old age the manifestation of the poverty of our human constitution? It is just not true that we get wiser. We get more stupid. Are the Jews then right when they celebrate the eightieth birthday as the day of entry into wisdom, as Lapide recently told me? If one forgets in old age, is that not an indoctrination into the *docta ignorantia* which one must have to be blessed? One can make something of becoming more stupid in old age. It occurs to me: not long ago I wrote a piece about old age for Vienna (I think for an education course) which is presumably not yet in my bibliography.[149] Kirchsläger could easily provide information about that and send it, because the whole of this theological correspondence course was about old age. Age is the manifestation of the *prolixitas mortis* of which Gregory the Great speaks. The present method of comforting the old with leisure-time occupations and easy sayings, important though these may be, is largely rubbish. I often think about death every day, and feel it in all my bones and thoughts. Why should I be disturbed about it? And the fear of death is really a good thing. No more occurs to me, If your doctoral student ever comes to the Tyrol (which would be very splendid), then she should drop in and I can talk to her about my experience of old age.

That's what Karl Rahner was like.

His eightieth birthday brought him great honours. On 11 and 12 February 1984 the Catholic Academy of Freiburg organized a conference in which he participated from beginning to end and, as alert and as sharp as ever, intervened in the discussions. The Auditorium Maximum of the University was filled to bursting. After that he went to give lectures in England and to the conference of the Budapest Academy which I have already mentioned. On 5 March, his actual birthday, he was fêted by the Jesuits of Innsbruck and the Theological Faculty there, the Tirol district and the city of Innsbruck. Lukas Vischer from the World Council of Churches gave the festal address. A Karl Rahner prize for the furthering of theological development was founded.

Three days after the celebrations Rahner became unwell. He suffered from difficulties in breathing and nose bleeds. The doctor ordered rest under medical supervision. From 9 to 29 March he was in the sanatorium of the Sisters of the Cross in Rum, near Innsbruck. After some days of rest he was given permission to take a daily walk with Frau Oeggl. After two attempts which ended with his favourite ice cream, it proved that the effort was too great. Rahner was out of breath, restless, and had no appetite, but he read, dictated to Frau Oeggl, among other things the letter which I have already mentioned to the bishops in Peru in which he asked for protection and understanding for Gustavo Gutierrez and the theology of liberation. Many Jesuits visited him. From 23 March on his state became visibly worse, and he suffered from lack of breath, unrest and retching. On 29 March he was taken into the University Medical Clinic in Innsbruck. Although he was very weak, he began a conversation with an orderly on whose uniform he had discovered the conscientious objectors' badge about his views. On entering his room at the clinic his first question was, 'Is there a telephone here and how do you use it?' In the evening a drip feed was attached to a vein; he watched the process in an alert way and made short, witty and wicked comments on it. After a very bad night, on Friday 30 March he was taken to the intensive care unit. There he lay with two othe patients in a room, attached to a blood-pressure monitor and drip feed machine which supplied liquid through the nose. Frau Oeggl held his hands. When towards evening his blood pressure got steadily worse, she called the hospital chaplain. He anointed Rahner, though Rahner gave no sign of being aware of it. Shortly afterwards the Rector of the Jesuit College, Fr Mullner, sat by Rahner's bedside and said some short prayers. Rahner opened his eyes, saw the Rector large and clear, and thanked him with a vigorous nod of the head. When asked whether he was in pain he shook his head. From then on he became increasingly more peaceful. Fr Walter Kern relieved the Rector, and he and Frau Oeggl stayed with Rahner. Late in the evening another woman who had long been a friend of his came into the room. The three watched with him. Rahner gave the impression of being relaxed, as though free from burdens and pressures. At 11.26 p.m. on 30 March 1984 he breathed his last.

In his prayer to God for recognition Karl Rahner had said:

> Then you will say the last word, the only word that abides and that one never forgets. Then, when all is silent in death and I have learned and suffered my last. Then will begin the great silence in which you alone resound, you who are Word from eternity to eternity. Then all human words will be dumb. Being and knowing, knowing and experiencing will be all the same: 'I will know as I am known', will understand what you have always said to me, namely yourself. No human word, no image and no concept will ever stand between me and you; you yourself will be the one joyful word of love and life that fills all the spheres of my soul.

Appendix

Karl Rahner

A Brief Correspondence from the Time of the Council

Between 1959 and 1965 Karl Rahner often commented in his letters to me on the Council or, more accurately, on his activity for the Council in general and for the renewal of the permanent diaconate in particular; on the imposition of the Roman preliminary censorship and its abolition; his difficulties with the church; and his wish to move from Innsbruck to Munich as Romano Guardini's successor. I published these comments from his letters in the Swiss journal Orientierung *in 1984 and am including them in this book,[1] because I was and am of the opinion that the texts give a clear idea of Rahner the man and the theologian, and that they are valuable to those who are interested in Rahner. A very wide response and indications of a desire to own the extracts in book form has confirmed that.*

This short correspondence is not a complete chronicle of, or commentary on, the Council, because there was constant opportunity for Rahner and me to converse between letters. It offers as it were just a sidelight on the scene.

The brackets () within the text mean that here I have omitted comments by Rahner which are purely private or do not relate to the themes I have just mentioned.

In Karl Rahner's letters to me I found an early comment on the aims of the Council as John XXIII had announced them on 25 January 1959:

I'm not surprised that hitherto in Rome it was thought in many circles that a council was no longer possible today. I was really half of this mind myself, purely for technical parliamentarian reasons. But if these difficulties can be overcome and really are overcome, then a new council could of itself achieve and represent a real dynamic force directed against the one-sided centralism in the church of the last few centuries, provided that we have enough bishops with a mind of their own. So we hope that the council will come to something.

Innsbruck, 17 February 1959

Rahner was appointed consultor *(adviser) to the 'Commission for the Discipline of the Sacraments' by John XXIII on 22 March 1961. This commission was led by Cardinal B.Aloisi Masella, and its secretary was R.Bidagor SJ. Among many other issues it had to work on the question of the restoration of the permanent diaconate, by presenting an outline to the central commission that was preparing for the Council. Together with the Yugoslavian archbishop F.Šeper, Rahner worked out an opinion which was included in the outline of the commission on the sacraments. He did this from Innsbruck; he was not invited to the sessions in Rome.*

Adviser to König and Döpfner

In October 1961, Franz König, Cardinal of Vienna, asked for Rahner's collaboration in looking through all the material that was intended for the central commission from the individual commissions:

I hear that on 8 December the Pope will announce the Council for autumn of next year. Cardinal König recently told me on the telephone that from now on he would like to send me the basic documents for the sessions of the central commission. I'm eager to see what they will be looking at there.

Innsbruck, 20 October 1961

Rahner felt that the preparatory texts were utterly unsatisfactory because the possibilities of a Council were not exhausted, and because they did not speak in any way the language that had to be spoken 'today'. So he began to write articles in various journals looking forward to the Council:

Simmel is taking my article on the Council.[2] That could be dangerous. It's to appear as early as February.

Innsbruck, 15 January 1962

My own article[3] is going well. () There will be a good deal in it that could not be found in the Roman opinion. I hope that it will meet your wishes.

Innsbruck, 19 January 1962

Rahner's preparation for the Council also included the editing of a collection on the renewal of the diaconate which he had undertaken at the request of the diaconate groups (Hannes Kramer and Josef Hornef) and was finishing with me.

As this book, Diaconia in Christo, *gradually became ready for the press, Rahner had the idea of dedicating it to an important figure at the Council in order to make him favourable towards the cause. First of all he thought of the President of the preparatory commission on the sacraments:*

As to the dedication, it will perhaps be best if I write (directly or indirectly?)[4] to Bidagor to ask him what he thinks of a dedication to Aloisi Masella. If he accepts this dedication, it can do no harm.

Innsbruck, 16 February 1962

To inform the cardinal what would be contained in the book, a Latin table of contents was sent to Rome. In the second half of January 1962 the sacrament commission's text was being considered by the Central Commission. The result was not known. In Osservatore Romano *there was a negative-sounding report which could mean one of two things: either that the voting in the central commission had gone badly for the renewal of the diaconate or that the author of the report wanted to do down the matter. Rahner commented:*

I've sent the Latin table of contents (many thanks for your pains) to Burkhart Schneider, so that he can give Bidagor some idea of our book. I don't know what note in *Osservatore Romano* is being talked about. I enquired of Schneider and asked him to ask Bidagor what it was about. If the schema sketched out by the sacrament commission has come to grief in the central commission, then *ipso facto* we have an objectively new situation, i.e. in that case our book no longer has the opportunity of being regarded as the basic book for these issues even after the Council, and perhaps the Cardinal will not accept the dedication so readily. But I don't know whether this history was already discussed at the central commission, far less what happened there. I must wait. If we do not win here, we shall at the next Council. At all events the book will be good, and must appear. It would be splendid if through your father we got enough copies to distribute it to all the bigwigs. As I've said, as long as I don't know what was in the *Osservatore* notice, I cannot very well go to the Cardinal with just one page, because I don't know what should be said on it. I'm now waiting for the report from Schneider. Then we'll see. We've still time. And I don't think that our book is coming out too late.

Innsbruck, 17 February 1962

Still no news from Burkhart Schneider. However, I've warned him again by someone who went to Rome on Tuesday. König has thanked me for my annotations on the material of the session of the central commission which is now being held. I'm dead tired. And quite exhausted.

Innsbruck, 21 February 1962

The following passage speaks for the first time about an Italian translation of the Concise Theological Dictionary *and sheds light on Rahner's position before the Council, above all in Italy.*

Scherer[5] has just written asking whether I am for or against an Italian translation of the little lexicon. Certainly Italian is a special problem because of the bigwigs and protectors of orthodoxy in Rome. That is why my *Schriften*, too, have not been translated into Italian. On the other hand, since this decision not to translate, my position has already been consolidated. One could also say that the little lexicon is written in such a way that these people will not understand it and therefore will not see what is said against its limitations. So I really don't know whether to say yes or no. Please see what you think. () As to the *Osservatore Romano*, I don't see what one could or should do in that direction. It doesn't really say anything. It seems to me that our answer will be our book. If people won't read that, then even a one-page comment will not get far. () As to the dedication, we can only wait. If the Cardinal does not want it, he leaves things as they are. Even then we're not in a bad position. The question would only be whether the ostensible reason is the true one, whether he is against the matter or just does not want to expose himself. – If a definite negative answer came from Rome, would we then offer Schäufele the dedication?[6] Is there anyone else who could be regarded as a protagonist for the diaconate?

Innsbruck, 22 February 1962

In answer to these questions I suggested to Rahner that the book should be dedicated to Cardinal Wyszyński, Primate of Poland, who was in regular contact with my father. It was then completely unknown how the Poles would react to central European theology and put their concerns to the Council. Rahner replied:

I've heard no more from Rome. So we must keep waiting. It would be splendid if the book could be dedicated to Wyszyński.

Innsbruck, 26 February 1962

The next comments express confidence and realism.

If the Romans are now unwilling over the diaconate, our book will be even more important. In that case it is all the more vital for the discussion to remain open. I could well imagine that a few years after the Council a Pope would allow at least certain bishops and areas to introduce the diaconate, precisely because the question has been left open. It is impossible to banish the fact that the first schema of the Council commission was for it. () If the Council does not feel that, we must just console Kramer and his men. But they will not have worked in vain. () I've still heard nothing from Schneider. I hope that no one in Rome is hatching a counter-blow at the book. These days anything is possible.

Innsbruck, 3 March 1962

Days later, a negative answer came from Burkhart Schneider, dated 1 March. Schneider wrote that Cardinal Aloisi Masella would not accept the dedication since '1. As President of the commission responsible for the matter he could not very well take up a position (and the acceptance of a dedication would at all events imply this), especially as some differences of opinion are to be expected at the Council itself; in addition there is the possibility or probability that the Cardinal may be considered as a possible future president of the Council and therefore he cannot bind himself in any way beforehand; 2. as the book is appearing in German and the cardinal is known not to have any German at all, he does not think it a good thing to accept the dedication of a book whose contents he knows only from a Latin translation of the table of contents and which he is not in a position to read.'

Rahner's reaction:

Negative letter from Schneider. All right, that's how it is. Question: will you invite the Polish cardinal? If you want to and have a way of doing it, carry on. If not, then we'll leave things for the moment. We can discuss later whether in that case we go to Schäufele. One idea: should we not see whether a Polish translation of the little lexicon could be arranged? That would mean more to me than an Italian translation: it would be good to have said something behind the Iron Curtain. I recently visited Luise Rinser. Her works are translated into Polish, so she has now been invited by a publisher there to make a journey to Poland. Think about it.

Innsbruck, 4 March 1962

He then gave the following news about work for the Council.

Next week I'm going to Hamburg for the lecture. I shall be away from Wednesday to Sunday. Before that, though, I have to do an opinion for König in Vienna. But the documents don't arrive until tomorrow.

Innsbruck, 7 March 1962

Again I have Council documents in front of me. They're less bad than the first lot.

Innsbruck, 9 March 1962

I hope the Cardinal of Warsaw says yes. I've already hatched a small plot over the same question to König. But that doesn't matter, it's only in case for some reason W. may not or cannot.

Innsbruck, 11 March 1962

It's night-time. I'm dead tired. Tomorrow I must begin to dictate the opinion for König and when that's done, read Küng.[7] It's a difficult time.

Innsbruck, 26 April 1962

I've finished my opinion for König. Thank God. It will be about thirty pages, mostly in Latin. Döpfner also wants it. Now I must get down to Küng's work as quickly as possible. The pestering doesn't stop. But it doesn't matter.

Innsbruck, 28 April 1962

It's night-time. I've just got back from Munich where I discussed Küng's book for seven hours with him and must do the same thing in Munich on 13 May. I think that we can confidently put König on the title page. Do a nice courteous dedication (German is quite all right) without being too devout. He has given me permission. As soon as he gets back from Rome or at the latest at the end of May in Salzburg[8] I shall write to him again or speak to him in person (in Salzburg). He certainly can't read the long Schmöker.

Innsbruck, 3 May 1962

The book is gigantic. Are 620 pages still not the end? () What kind of serious studies have appeared for the Council? I know of nothing except this book.

Innsbruck, 9 May 1962

I'm really rather proud of the diaconate book.

Innsbruck, 14 May 1962

Again I got from König such a packet of Council material that yesterday I said no to Venice.[9] All the time I have available for work for König is the week before Pentecost, and on Whitsunday the session of the Central Commission begins again. () We should now be finally clear about the dedication of the *Diaconia*. I want to tell König myself what the dedication is before it appears. – I'm really proud of the diaconate book, even if it is rather long,

or precisely because it is. There are few books in the church which
discuss a living problem thoroughly and exactly.

Innsbruck, 19 May 1962

Schillebeeckx is not being thrown out. Marlet, who spoke with
him a few days ago, told me. He's going to Rome with Alfrink in
October, which is also very good for me.[10] () König also wrote a
friendly letter to me again. Yesterday he sailed off to Rome. Is
there still no reply from Poland?

Innsbruck, May 1962

Preliminary censorship, further work

*While Karl Rahner was working on like this for the Council,
without warning and with no reasons given, Rome ordered that
his writing should undergo a special preliminary censorship.*

Pentecost. Seven o'clock in the morning. Warmest wishes for
Pentecost. () I've now got stupid troubles with Rome again. In
future they want me to submit everything that I write to a Roman
preliminary censorship, like de Lubac and Congar (do they still
have to do this? I don't know). I've already said that in that case
I shall simply stop writing (and thought to myself: in that case
from now on I shall be called Vorgrimler, Metz or Darlap). I've
already given the alarm to König, Döpfner, Volk and Höfer in a
long letter.[11] We'll see if they can do anything. I imagine that the
matter comes from the Holy Office and that the General is only
an intermediary. Please (I beg you) don't say anything about it to
anyone for the moment;[12] because when it comes to telling the
story publicly, I must keep my powder intact and dry. I only heard
last Thursday, without any reason being given. More later. At
Trinity, van Gestel[13] is coming here for the four hundredth
anniversary of the college. I shall probably hear more then. I'll
pass it on to you either by letter or by word of mouth. How's the
Flemish book getting on?[14] (It would be very amusing if I could
throw that in these people's faces, but it won't be ready yet.)

Innsbruck, 10 June 1962

Gestel's here at the moment. I haven't really been able to talk
to him yet. Tomorrow will be the first opportunity. However, he

has already stressed in passing that nothing can be done in our Curia, but that it all happened under heavy pressure from the office. (Of course he hinted at more.) König telephoned that he would do something in Rome. Volk has written to me that he will try to get Frings moving on the case. I have told König that he should have a go at Ottaviani. How energetic he is about it is, of course, another question. Höfer has not reacted yet, nor Döpfner. Furthermore, attempts will be made, if the matter is not simply reversed, if possible to get 'Roman' censors here in the country (e.g. in Frankfurt). Of course this is only of use if these have civil courage. Which one should expect. You needn't worry. I shan't resign. There will be a fight. (I recently heard that the Romans are saying of the constitution *Veterum sapientia*[15], 'Veterum, si; sapientia, no'). Don't worry. Pray for me. God very readily hears prayers of rage. Because he is with those of lively hearts.

Innsbruck, 15 June 1962

Rahner went to Rome to discuss the matter with the Jesuit General himself.

Early yesterday I got back from Rome, having travelled there over Thursday night. The cardinals were no longer there. This afternoon I'm going to talk with Döpfner in Munich before my lecture there. König telephoned me here on Sunday but didn't catch me; he didn't ring again yesterday, though he had promised. But I know that he discussed my case with the Pope personally. The Pope is said to have asked him to take up the matter in writing with full documentation, with the HO[16] or with him (?), and to have regretted the whole thing. We shall see if we get any further. Our General was very nice and really amazingly cordial. He told me that the action comes just from the HO; he has nothing against me, he regrets having such tasks to perform where no reasons are given; he has asked for the reasons but has received either no answer at all or nothing that conveys anything. He gave examples. He has nothing against my having mobilized König and Döpfner, one of whom has already spoken with him on the matter. He also recommended that I should involve Frings. I said that I would visit him in July when I would be in the Rhineland anyway. Nor does he have anything against my bringing out Vol.V of the *Schriften* outside this statute, because the matter is already arranged with Benziger and the contents have already been through censorship (Schasching and Coreth were involved).[17]

I've also spoken with Höfer and he's spoken with the cardinals. Of course it's hard to say whether he was able to have a good go at them. Still, the battle is not yet lost.

I also told the General (and he did not contradict me) that I had no intention of submitting anything to the Roman censorship but would rather write nothing at all; nor would I keep quiet about the matter, but would describe it all quite candidly, and those who had aspersions cast on them as a result would be others than me. He did not protest against that either. It was conceded that in the long run I couldn't keep the matter quiet, since many people knew about it already. – Now I have an idea which I want to pass on to you before I tell anyone else. Please give me your frank opinion about it. Would it be conceivable that one could send an address to the Pope (in Italian and in German) in which (courteously, very courteously, but clearly) there was a protest against this muzzling, mainly or solely signed by lay people and handed over or sent to the Pope? One would have to indicate the cause, have some friendly words about my 'services', supported by facts, about how these signatories were acquainted with me, and ask for the abolition of this unjust measure which harmed and damaged the reputation of the church in Germany. () The only question is how one could do that relatively quickly, so that all the signatures were collected at least during August. One would need a good number of names; not too many, but important ones. (People like Krone[18], who knows me, and so on would be there from the start.) () I wouldn't want to suggest to whom else one might go. However, we could consider the text together. It must be short and clear, so that it is also read in Rome; it must be of such a kind that the people to whom one goes for their signature see at first glance that they can happily add their names to it and should do if they are not cowardly. One would have to think of how to work things that a large number of names were collected quickly. However, the basic question is of course whether this makes sense and is in fact necessary. I'm not really concerned for myself. I would even be happy to spend a couple of years writing quietly for myself and publishing it later. () But my feeling its that we should not make things too easy for these terrible bigwigs. If they come up against resistance they will at least be more careful next time and think harder. Today they are shooting at de Lubac, Congar, Chenu, Lyonnet, Zerwick (the last two are again not yet out of the wood and only in the case of Fuchs[19] has the HO been defeated), then myself; others will follow later. This new integralism must be fought in every possible way. That's what I'm concerned about; hence this idea. If it proves to be a new one, good; in that case it may make more of an impression. Once I know how things stand with Döpfner or König I'll tell you and that will also throw new light on this idea. () I think that the time has not yet come to make a great stir about the matter. But as far as I'm concerned there is no need for it to be kept secret.

Unfortunately I don't know who denounced me to the HO. () According to Höfer, a short while ago there was nothing in the acts; he was told this by a man who knows these acts. Do they want to stop my mouth before the Council? Alfrink is furious that the Italian translation of the Pastoral Letter from all the Dutch bishops about the Council had to be withdrawn from the shops on the instructions of the HO to the Turin Salesian General (the thing was printed by the Salesians). However, it is said that things went very badly for Ottaviani at the last session of the central commission over his schema on the Catholic state and its task as the secular arm of the church.

Innsbruck, 26 June 1962

So on Tuesday I was with Döpfner and on Thursday with König. The present situation is that Döpfner, König and Frings (who has already declared his support) will make a written statement to the Pope asking for the abolition of this preliminary censorship of me in Rome. König, who has to write it, has told me that I should do an outline of the text with Schasching, and Schasching should then bring him the text and discuss it with him. I said that the matter had already been raised by word of mouth (recently in the audiences with König and Döpfner) so that we should not be in too much of a hurry. It could be arranged that I have also spoken personally with Frings before the statement is presented in the second half of July. Our General has recommended this. Whether anything will come out of this whole situation is another matter. General Döpfner is also rather pessimistic about the matter. So my question to you about the lay petition in my last letter takes on a new aspect: have we enough time to do both things more or less simultaneously or even together? Would that make sense? Of course I've said nothing to König and Döpfner about this plan. () I wonder whether we should not also seek signatures from theological colleges at the universities? Here we must certainly be careful that there isn't a leak and that someone advises Rome and the HO before we have collected the addresses. But it could be that if we could get some signatures at a university through a helpful man, other supporters would join in (particularly if one told them that with three cardinals they would be in good company) and would blame themselves and think it suspicious if they didn't join in. So think about things again and let me know. () I'll tell you anything else I've heard from Döpfner, etc., by word of mouth; it's not very elevating.

Innsbruck, 29 June 1962

If you still have it, could you give me again the material that I sent you for your Flemish book on me? Perhaps I can get some dates and numbers from it without having to dig them out again for the statement to the Pope from Cardinal König that Schasching and I have to make for him. Presumably they will expect some praise for me, even if it's only brief, and for this some figures (other than those about the bibliography) are the simplest and most convincing.

Innsbruck, 29 June 1962 (second letter)

You can see the problem in my case very accurately. If these bigwigs still feel too powerful, such a petition can have the opposite effect from the one that we imagine. I've thought about your letter again. At all events, let's wait to see how the action of the cardinals goes. If nothing comes of it, then we can always start the other action. () Bettschart has just been here.[20] He wants to bring out Vol. V before Christmas. It will be about 550 pages long (I did not think that I had produced so much since October 1960). So if we have no success I can even write nothing for a while. () Don't worry, it's not worth the effort. We mustn't give these people the pleasure of getting annoyed at us. Just think what someone once said in the Nazi barracks to an anti-Nazi: only those who respect you can hurt you.

Innsbruck, 2 July 1962

Meanwhile it was even broadcast on the radio that Rahner was prohibited from writing and speaking. The representatives of the Paulusgesellschaft of their own accord started a petition among those at their conferences who were interested in the affair. About 250 figures, including a large number of lecturers in the natural sciences, joined in this petition to the Pope.[21] Rahner wrote:

One may not assert what is not the case. And unfortunately they have not just forbidden me to write but imposed a preliminary censorship of an extraordinary kind in Rome. And so far there hasn't been a prohibition against lecturing and so on. () I knew nothing about K.'s enterprise. I only heard about it once it had already started. I warned him by letter and telephone to be careful and not to do more harm than good. () K. has let fly before having exact details about the case, as I discovered from him yesterday in a telephone conversation. And of course that doesn't make things any better. What shall I do? We'll discuss this further in Freiburg.

Innsbruck, 9 July 1962

In this situation the idea first occurred to Rahner that a move to a West German university could give him more freedom. Münster had put out the first feelers in his direction. He wrote:

I'm seriously wondering whether I shouldn't write to the General in Rome that he should let me go to Münster. Granted, that might not perhaps be much use. But who knows that before the answer? But should I? What do you think? If you want to, have time, and have thoughts on the problem, do write to me.

Innsbruck, 31 July 1962

Martini's lay letter[22] and so on over the Roman censorship has to go to Rome; a few days ago I received a copy with about 250 names which make it very good. I'm sending this copy to the General in Rome and also mentioning the offer from Münster in the accompanying letter in roughly the same way as you also think that this is a way of exerting pressure. I wonder whether it will do any good? ()

Otherwise I've heard nothing about the Roman matter. The Pope is very ill. How will that affect the Council? They said that

all the schemata together would amount to more than 2000 pages!
How will they cope with that?

Brixen, 14 August 1962

*In the meantime Cardinal Wyszyński had written to me that he
would gladly accept the dedication in the book on the diaconate.*
Diaconia in Christo *appeared before the Council and was dedicated jointly to Cardinals Wyszyński and König.*

Yesterday evening I got back from Hanover.[23] I think it all went
well there. Döpfner was at my lecture to about 800 (I guess) clergy,
and afterwards was very complimentary. So was Hengsbach. ()
The General sent me a telegram to Hanover: *tomus quintus edi
potest.* So that's all right. I don't know whether anything has
come of Cardinal Bea's conversation with the Pope[24] in which he
promised 'to find ways' of satisfying their Eminences and me. I
still don't have a real decision in the censorship story. One can
hope cautiously. Bea was also in Hanover. We talked a little in a
friendly but guarded way, without saying anything substantial.

Munich, 26 August 1962

*This summer too, as usual, Rahner spent several weeks in Freiburg,
above all to work on the* Lexikon für Theologie und Kirche. *At
this time he also wrote some articles for Vol.VII. Archbishop
Schäufele worked hard in Rome to obtain consent that the
censorship of the church in Freiburg would be enough for these
articles, and that the special Roman censorship did not apply. He
was given this consent. Rahner wrote:*

I'm still in Munich. () Here I've been preparing the endless
Council histories for the sessions with Volk. () With the Pope it's
a matter that concerns me. I also find it very ambivalent that the
HO is so gracious over *LTK*. Is this a payment on account to the
Pope and the Cardinals, after which there will be no more? I've
told Döpfner and written to Schäufele that I'm afraid of that and
that the concession over *LTK* is not great, since I could very easily
have found help elsewhere. But I will see how things go in Rome.
Next Sunday I'm going to Vienna. There I have to give a lecture
to the conference of the International Children's Villages (to
oblige Gmeiner), then on 2 October I return to Innsbruck; on 7

October I have to marry Bernd Bultmann in Salzburg and on the 8th I have a lecture in Graz. After that I travel to Rome.

Munich, 24 September 1962

The Council, first period

On 11 October 1962, Pope John XXIII solemnly opened the Second Vatican Council with remarks which made it clear that he did not want any mere repetition of dogmatic and moral formulae nor any condemnations. What would happen to the dogmatic outlines on the 'sources' of revelation, the deposit of faith (the depositum fidei*), the church and Mary (*De BMV*), which had the blessing of the central commission? Would the texts on chastity and so on which had similar authorization go through the Council without discussion?*

The first two General Assemblies on 13 and 16 October were concerned with the procedures for voting on the Council commissions. Rahner wrote to me from Rome:

So far at any rate things at the Council have not gone as Ottaviani and Co. had expected. That offers some little hope. But only when we get to the actual subject-matter will we be able to see whether the people who want to do more than repeat and defend are sufficiently numerous for the Council to have some prospects. In the last week I have spoken for three-quarters of an hour to the German, Austrian and Swiss bishops on the second[25] dogmatic schema. Really the same as if I were saying something to you. Frings presided over the Assembly. At the end of this slaughter he said that he agreed with everything and that discussion was really superfluous. And no one contradicted him. What would Schäufele have thought of that? () Of course the whole thing here goes on with a good many undercurrents, discussions and machinations.

Still, one also gets to know some interesting people. () Otherwise apart from the endless consultations in smaller and very small groups (this afternoon, for example a good dozen German and French theologians are meeting with Volk; Schmaus will not be there because he's gone back to Germany, and we didn't invite Schauf[26]) I've been plaguing myself over a preliminary sketch for a new dogmatic schema so that we have something different and positive to offer when we attempt to bring down Tromp's outlines.[27]

It's doubtful whether I have any prospect of joining in the dogmatic commission as a *peritus*. Intrinsically I've none. For according to the previous procedure, only the president of the commission has the right to introduce a *peritus*. And Ottaviani will certainly never make me one. But attempts will be made to change the procedure on this particular point. All the bishops in the above assembly were in favour of this change (thus including Frings, Döpfner and König). I said to the Strasbourg coadjutor yesterday when he visited me that he should also bring in the French bishops, and he promised to try to do that. One can only hope that he achieves something. And be patient.

Rome, 19 October 1962

There's really nothing to report from here which is not also in the newspapers. Yesterday was the first session on the decree on the liturgy. The one who fought hardest against it was the secretary of the Congregation of Rites. Yet generally the mood towards the decree seems favourable. Yes, it's certainly very tame, but it's the least that one can expect. On Friday I'm flying to Munich till Saturday. – We've already made very good friends with the more progressive French. The French seem to have become better than one might have expected after their contributions to the central commission and earlier. – And a little anecdote: Lubac's book on Teilhard passed the censorship of the HO. But hardly had it appeared than it was attacked shabbily in the *Osservatore*. *Orientierung* also got a *miramur* because of its article on Latin in church. I'm eager to see what will happen to mine.[28] Still, it's good to be alive when one has nothing to lose and does not want to become a prelate or the like.

Rome, 22 October 1962

In October 1962 Karl Rahner was nominated by the Pope as a peritus, *i.e. an official Council theologian. In this capacity he got a pass which entitled him to take part in the General Assemblies of the Council (the Plenum in St Peter's). These assemblies interested him only because of the voting and not because of the speeches in which the bishops read out what their theologians had given them. As* peritus *Rahner did not yet have the right to take part in sessions of the commissions. That is where the decisive work was done through the collaboration of bishops and theologians: the formulation of basic texts. Rahner was interested in collaborating on the Theological Commission in which the dogmatic themes (church, revelation) were being discussed:*

It is still very uncertain whether I shall get into the theological commission. Granted, König is in it, but according to earlier procedure which still has not been changed, only Ottaviani can introduce a *peritus*. I also think that he will refuse König if he attempts to bring me in with him. At the moment there is great excitement here among the Council people about the choice of the members of the commissions nominated by the Pope. In this way Dante has come into the commission on liturgy, the man who made an absolutely stupid speech in the Council assembly against the schema and the use of the vernacular in the liturgy. Similarly, Parente[29] has found his way into the theological commission. More than a third of these new members are Italians and Spaniards. In addition there are some from the USA (probably reactionary). It is remarkable how the South Americans seem to be more progressive, whereas the Americans and the English usually seem to be extremely reactionary. I don't go to the sessions of the Plenum on the liturgy. That would be a waste of time. I'm struggling over attempts at schemata which Ratzinger and I, Congar and Philips are working on.[30] They will probably be no good to anyone. Still, there really are a large number of people who hate the schemata of Hürth and Tromp and fight against them, so there's hope yet. We must press on as best we can. One cannot yet say (signs of weariness are already appearing) when the liturgy schema will be finished or when there will be proper votes. I don't yet know what will then emerge from the dogmatics (*De fontibus revelationis*, etc., or even *De Ecclesia* first). That's very stupid because one doesn't know what to concentrate on. () I get on well with Ratzinger. And he is very much in Frings' good books.

Rome, 30 October 1962

Your biography of me has also come. Very many thanks; I'm extremely touched. Of course I can't promise when I shall read it, because I'm not very interested in myself. But anyhow I'm very glad about the book, since it's a sign that the theology that I try to put forward cannot be suppressed completely, but is a hope that it is slowly making progress (I hope not too late). I also notice here that I'm not yet all that old, even when I sit at a table with Daniélou, Congar, Ratzinger, Schillebeeckx and so on. I find that these still do not realize clearly enough how little, e.g. a christology 'from above', which simply begins with the declaration that God has become man, can be understood today. And the same is true in so many other instances. Of course one can hardly expect that another way of thinking will already make a mark on the schemata of the Council, but I do not find it explicitly enough among the progressive theologians themselves. Otherwise there's not much to report from here. I don't go to the sessions. () In the morning I have to go to Frings. Ratzinger and I are to present him with the 'schema' that we've sweated over. It's a very innocent affair and has virtually no prospect of really being debated at the Council. But one must do what one can to overthrow the official schemata. Philips of Louvain has produced a similar schema on the church and Congar a kind of preface in the form of a confession of faith. Daniélou has attempted to tailor a new garment from scraps of the official schemata. I'm impatient to see how things will develop. We still don't know what is coming after the schema on the liturgy. But the inclination after that to begin on the *Ecclesia* schema seems to be growing. It is said that already ten cardinals are in favour. That would be good, and in that case there would be an increasing prospect of certain other schemata of a theological kind being consigned to the silence of the tomb. You will have heard that according to the Luxembourg paper Alfrink recently stopped Ottaviani because he was speaking too long and that people then began to clap (which otherwise is not usual). Motto: Schadenfreude is the purest joy. Ottaviani is said to be asking everyone in the HO why people hate him so much. And Parente has already declared himself to be a martyr of the HO.

Rome, 5 November 1962

So this week the dogmatics is beginning here. I'm eager to see what happens, but I don't have great hopes. Recently I wrote a Latin counter-opinion on the first dogmatic schema. This afternoon all the German bishops were given it. The German speakers have produced 400 copies of it in fine style.[31] Tomorrow I have to give a lecture to the South American bishops. Perhaps we shall collect a good one-third minority, which can prevent the worst. Frings is optimistic. Others like me are less so. *Videbimus*. Frings is also circulating about 2000 copies of a kind of schema which Ratzinger and I have produced. In my view its prospects are nil.

When will Vol. VII appear? I'd like to know soon, so that perhaps I can give copies to a few people here. Perhaps to Ottaviani, who no longer comes to the sessions, furious because they made him stop speaking. But now that dogmatics is beginning he will come again and act as a proper Pope.

Rome, 12 November 1962

The great turning point came on 21 November 1962: John XXIII had the prepared outline on the 'sources of revelation' withdrawn. He appointed a mixed commission with Ottaviani and Bea as presidents to produce a new text on divine revelation. In this way it was decided that the Council did not simply have to accept the Roman texts which had to be prepared for it. On 1 December the discussion of the text De Ecclesia, *on the church, began in the Plenum.*

At present they're discussing *De Ecclesia* in the Plenum. I've made a commentary on it which is being circulated in an edition of 1300 copies. I've already sent it to you. It is still uncertain whether we shall secure a rejection of the schema as in the case of *De fontibus revelationis*. More uncertain than in the case of the first schema. Today I'm at last to go with König to a session of the commission which is to make a new schema to replace the one that has fallen through.[32] () D. went away again today. He was there a very long time. That was very good for me, because he wrote both the opinion on *De BMV* and the counter-opinion against *De Ecclesia* on matrices so I don't have to go begging round the German speakers who saw to producing the thing. All in all we have printed about 50,000 sheets with all the equipment here. When we add the Ratzinger-Rahner schema to that it will be even more (that has been 'printed' by Frings in the Anima).

Rome, 5 December 1962

Karl Rahner's doubts as to whether Cardinal Ottaviani would exclude him from the work of the commission were proved wrong.

Cardinal König's courage came out on top. Ottaviani accepted Rahner as an adviser on the theme of revelation:

This afternoon I must go again with König to the session of the mixed commission on reworking the schema that has fallen through. This afternoon will be delicate.

Rome, 7 December 1962

However, many bishops also wanted the text on the church to be redone. Along with others, including his Frankfurt colleague Otto Semmelroth SJ, Bishop Volk's conciliar theologian, Rahner was invited to work on a new outline:

Immediately after Christmas Semmelroth and Co. will come to Munich, where we shall then (perhaps also with Schmaus) have to brood on the Council schema *De Ecclesia* for the German bishops, who need it by February.

Innsbruck, 17 December 1962

Rahner felt so fortified by these repeated indications of episcopal trust that he even forgot the Roman preliminary censorship. When I told him that the Jesuits of Lyons had invited me to join in the work on the Festschrift for H.de Lubac and gave him my theme, he wrote:

I congratulate you on the idea (theme) of the de Lubac article. It's good. It reminds me that I too must do something (and forget the Roman censorship). () We still haven't finished the schema for Munich. But it won't be long. I'm going to Munich on Sunday. We hear that recently in Rome the co-ordinating commission has completely rejected the schemata *De deposito fidei pure custodiendo* and *De castitate* etc, so that these themes will not come up at all. That would be splendid.

On the way in Rhineland, 1 January 1963

I got back from Munich last week. Over the last week we had two-day discussions with the German bishops about the schema *De Ecclesia* which we cooked up and the criticism of the Roman scheme which Semmelroth had once again consolidatd after our criticisms in Rome. Despite vigorous opposition from Schauf, the bishops really moved over entirely to our line. Of course, whether it will be any good in Rome is quite another matter. Still, Elchinger of Strasbourg believes that we will get the support of a good many French bishops, since they are against the old scheme but no new counter-proposal can be made in France. The regrettable result of Munich was that I have to go to Rome next Sunday evening. For various commission sessions begin there then, both on the schema *de revelatione* and on the schema *de Ecclesia*. There's a great deal of pressure, since everything has to be sufficiently far on by 10 March to be presented again to the bishops outside. This deadline seems to me to be utopian. But it does mean that it is highly unlikely that I can get back to Innsbruck before 10 March, especially as it is hardly likely that other German theologians will be available in Rome. For as far as I know, only König, Schröffer and Volk are on this commission in addition to Frings. As Schröffer has asked me to instruct him beforehand, it seems that he's not bringing a theologian with him. Nor do I think that Semmelroth is going, especially as at present he seems to me to be very sick and inactive. To this extent I have no alternative but to go to Rome.

Innsbruck, 11 February 1963

In the first part of the next letter Rahner mentions an enquiry which had just reached him from Munich as to whether he would be prepared to follow Romano Guardini at the university there. In the second paragraph he goes back to talking about the diaconate, which was so dear to his heart.

In the next few days (on Monday) I shall sound out van Gestel to see whether anything can be done. Höfer will back me up if he has to. Everything will depend on how far the Munich cardinal puts this idea to our generation, i.e. how energetic he is. Personally he's probably for it. I recently had a short conversation with him in Munich on the subject.

Tell Hannes Kramer that he should go on hoping and praying that the diaconate business progresses as far as it can in present circumstances. I'm enclosing two texts from two schemata on the church (in which one cannot of course say much about the church as it is, because this is a dogmatic scheme, of such a kind that not much can be said in favour of the diaconate in proportion, especially if one hopes to get it through). One text is mine (in the schema of the German bishops), the other is from Parente's new scheme; he has quite openly (although elsewhere he is very Trompian and reactionary) copied from me, i.e. from the German scheme. You can tell Kramer that. Of course he has to be discreet; he can hope, but he must also be sober and cautious. The practical regulations in canon law are not a matter for dogmatic theologians. I also doubt whether any will be made at this stage. But at least we have a peg to hang things on in future, if what has been said can remain in the dogmatic schema. And then it may well very soon become praxis. There is in fact less about the diaconate in the outline of a schema on the church from the Chilean bishops than there is in ours, because the indication that more could happen is really missing. But it's mentioned in that schema as well.

Rome, 23 February 1963

The text on revelation and the text on the church were discussed in parallel.

Yesterday there was again a session from 4 until almost 8. Contrary to expectations, things went very well, so we may expect that nothing will be said about the exact relationship between scripture and tradition (despite the howling of Tromp, Ottaviani, Schauf, Ruffini, Balic and so on). This time Bea has done things better, but he has also had some luck. Of course we shall only be over the hill when the Council's finished. This afternoon there is a private discussion with the French (König, etc.) on the *Ecclesia* schema. I can't imagine how it will get done soon enough. I wrote some other things yesterday. () So tomorrow I shall probably talk for the first time with Gestel about Munich.

Rome, 23 February 1963

During this stay in Rome, Rahner learned two important things. He heard that Cardinal Ottaviani was thinking of lifting the preliminary censorship and he was officially appointed peritus *in a new commission:*

It seems that the HO has begun to retreat on the matter of my censorship. However, I still have to hear more. Presumably there will be a desire to save face here, so we shall see what happens in practice. More later. I am now officially in a *periti* commission of seven men (I'm the only German) who are in effect to make a new schema *de Ecclesia* on the basis of the work of Philips of Louvain, taking other schemata into account (including the German one that we did). As the whole thing is to be brief, especially as there is virtually no time, we shall not be able to do anything very clever (even if things go peacefully: there is also someone from the HO and from Balic[33] in it). But perhaps we shall be able to prevent bad things which were in the official scheme and at least make some sensible contributions from a distance. Of course there is the question whether anything of what we seven achieve gets through the Faith Commission proper. – In an interval during a wild session in which there was an almighty row I had a conversation with Ottaviani – actually about my case. What I had heard from van Gestel on Monday (see above) was also told me again in substance.[34] Ottaviani was really very friendly. At all events there will be no more danger of my not getting into a session. But I must tell you all these stories again when we meet. At all events, you needn't worry that I'm giving in. I'm the only one who intervenes 'briefly' in the sessions, which has already provoked the amazement of Parente. I was the only one of five *periti* to speak out against the opinion of Ottaviani in a session in which the faith commission was without the Bea people. This evening Archbishop Hurley of South Africa is coming to see me. Balic begged me to do something (said I was the most powerful man) to see that a theological conference is held on scripture and tradition, which is his proposal. And so on. I would be very glad to go to Munich. What do you think of this story? However, here in our Curia no one is very enthusiastic about this idea. They think that Innsbruck is more important. But of course Döpfner wasn't there yet. And I'm avoiding provoking a negative answer which people later will be reluctant to take back.

Rome, 27 February 1963

It is clear from this text that the structure of work at the Council was rather complicated. The real members of the commissions were bishops. Periti were attached to them. Rahner was partly active for the faith commission, i.e. for the bishops who had to edit the dogmatic outlines – in this phase, the text on the church.

He also worked for the mixed commission made up of members of the faith commission and members of the Oecumene commission; he calls the latter 'Bea people' here. In this mixed commission the text on revelation was to be reworked. Here he represented the standpoint which had been confirmed by the researches of the Tübingen theologian J.R.Geiselmann: that even earlier Council decisions like those of Trent do not compel Catholics to assume a second 'source of revelation', oral tradition, alongside Holy Scripture.

Today should be (after a setback: session with a tremendous row in which Bea behaved well) the session in which there is a vote on the passage 'scripture-tradition'. Presumably it will end with the acceptance of a formula which doesn't say much. It doesn't matter. Even so we (the firm of Geiselmann and Co.) shall have in fact won, because nothing will be said against us. In the seven-*periti*-commission we have redone *De Ecclesia*. Nothing world-shattering has emerged. But Philips is confident that when the outline is ready it will be accepted by the faith commission of the bishops.

Rome, 1 March 1963

Van Gestel hasn't said no to my going to Munich, but of course he has promised very much less. He said that the General is not much in favour. Now everything will depend on whether and how intensively Döpfner supports me. We shall have to wait. Even Höfer thought that with Balthasar I was the only one who could be considered. () Yesterday afternoon there was another sitting of the mixed commission until nearly eight in the evening. After Bea once again completely messed up the matter to begin with, it seems to me that in the end things have turned out well. However, the revelation schema will not have passed the commission completely until Monday. And until that has happened I'm still wary. For the Ottaviani people keep exploding new mines. Yesterday I intervened four times – three times only very briefly. But on one occasion at some length and powerfully, right at the beginning of the discussion of what was really the most tricky point (as first *peritus*): I said that of course the most worthy fathers could accept the version of the new text, but in all modesty I would like to draw their attention to the fact that the new wording said in different terms precisely what in an earlier session it had been resolved, with a two-thirds majority, *not* to say. I think that this bomb hit the target very well. For Bea, who at that time had laudably arranged this two-thirds majority, had already declared himself in agreement with the new text.

Rome, 2 March 1963

During the revision of the text on the church Rahner constantly had the question of the diaconate in mind. Referring to a future stay in Freiburg, he wrote:

Would it make sense if on this occasion I made a short Latin exposition of the need to retain the passage on the diaconate in the *Ecclesia* scheme and sent this exposition along with the diaconate book to all members of the faith commission before it meets in the middle of May (if someone can make it financially possible to provide these copies)? In that case the book would probably make more sense. () What do you think? Talk to Kramer if you have time. At any rate, I've done all I can over this matter.

Innsbruck, 19 March 1963

I spoke with Döpfner last Sunday and asked him urgently to keep an eye on the matter of the diaconate in the co-ordinating commission. (Moreover he has already written to our General over my Munich business, though I don't know whether he has done so urgently enough; I told him that he should also go in person. I wonder whether he will?).

Innsbruck, 25 March 1963

With this I'm sending you the text of the covering letter which I've already done to send with the diaconate books. I wanted to do it here so that perhaps, if possible, it can be duplicated by Kramer in Freiburg and I can sign it there straight away. Then we can get on with things directly. () In the letter I was not quite sure what style to use when addressing cardinals and bishops at the same time. I think that it would be better (if that doesn't present too many technical problems) if in some copies only their Eminences were addressed and in others just the Excellencies (in the singular). So different things would have to be said in the address and at the end. () I've written a quite angry letter to van

Gestel and asked very, very urgently to be allowed to go to Munich. It's got so Austrian again here that I really would like to go. Martini will get Frings to sing the same song. I wonder whether he will do anything and whether it will be any use? Döpfner has written on the matter. I wonder whether he will also intercede orally in Rome? The South German Provincial is also writing to support me. Wait and see.

Innsbruck, 30 March 1963

I've still heard nothing about Munich from Rome. The Provincial still hasn't condescended to tell me what happened with the HO over the censorship business. Today König has telephoned from Vienna that the faith commission will continue in Rome on 16 May and that I must quite certainly come. Philips of Louvain has now also sent the first two chapters of the *Ecclesia* schema once again. Now it's yes. At any rate they have also met with the approval of the co-ordinating commission in Rome, as even Tromp writes to Philips. In a few days König will be sending me the text (which the faith commission has not yet approved) of chs.3 and 4 of the *Ecclesia* scheme, so that we can comment on it in advance in writing if we want to. In Philips ch.2 the passage on the diaconate is still there. And it is said in a note that it should only come out if something is said about the matter by the Council elsewhere. But as this is not to be expected, it is to be hoped that we can really get this passage through in May. But it will be good if the books and my letter go off soon. We shouldn't neglect any possibility at this point in time.

Innsbruck, 8 April 1963

König has sent new material from the schemata. The thing on church and modern culture seems to me to have been badly done by Daniélou and I find it a hideous mess. To be modern in this way with cheap remarks is worse than being old-fashioned and solid. Or so I think.

Innsbruck, 11 April 1963

In his personal life during these years Karl Rahner was troubled by what had happened to his brother Hugo, whose illness eventually prevented him from teaching.

Still silence from Rome (even Coreth) over the Munich business.

But I take that as a favourable sign. Now I would be very happy if I could take Hugo with me to Munich. I'm writing today, as Simmel suggested, to see whether he could possibly have Hugo in his new house which is to be begun in May, if Hugo would sort things out here.

Innsbruck, 12 April 1963

Still nothing from Rome. Not even about what has been done over the censorship business. In a day or so I shall tell Coreth that unless I do not hear something over this last matter soon, I shall tell the Paulusgesellschaft people in Salzburg that nothing has changed and that they can make a fuss in Rome, which I have called off.

Innsbruck, 14 April 1963

Today I was sent from France a nice review of the first part of *Mission et Grâce* by Richaud, Cardinal of Bordeaux. Not the sort of thing that we find in Germany. Two impressions of the book were sold out there in six months.[35] A third is coming out. And the second part (or book) is now being printed. In it the individual passages are prefaced with brief introductions by the translator. I've told him that in the article on the diaconate he is to refer to the big diaconate book. Otherwise there's no news. I've still not finished the opinion for König, but tomorrow night I must go to Vienna. Still nothing from Rome.

Innsbruck, 21 April 1963

In the meantime twenty-seven copies of *Diaconia in Christo* were sent to the cardinals and bishops of the Council commission for the doctrine of faith and morals with Rahner's accompanying letter, and the thanks came in at the end of April. Some commented at least briefly on the problem; others were formal and did not say anything. I would like to include three of them in this documentation.

Sacrosanctum Oecumenicum Concilium Vaticanum II
Commissio de doctrina fidei et morum
E Civitate Vaticana, 27 April 63

Dear Pater Rahner,
In the name of His Eminence Cardinal Ottaviani I thank you warmly for the *Quaestiones disputatae de Diaconia* and the

covering letter. Yesterday evening I personally received the book and the letter: many thanks for your kindness. His Eminence assumes that you have sent the book to all the bishops on our commission. If that is not the case, His Eminence is prepared to have the covering letter duplicated and brought to the attention of our commission.

You know my view. We should begin with mission; otherwise, in fact we shall achieve nothing.

With many greetings and best wishes,

Frater in Christo, Sebastian Tromp SJ

26 April 1963

Dear Pater Rahner

Today I received the book *Diaconia in Christo* and thank you for it very much. I have no difficulties over the renewal of the diaconate as a *ministerium* in the Latin church. My only hesitation is over whether it should be with or without celibacy. That is the big question.

With religious devotion to Our Lord,

Michael Cardinal Browne, OP

Archiepiscopus Zagrebiensis
Zagreb, 22 April 1963

Dear Pater,

It was a pleasant surprise when today's post brought me *Diaconia in Christo*. My deepest thanks for your kindness. It is truly a capital work and a real enyclopaedia on the problem. I have fought strongly for the cause in the preparatory commission. It would be a good thing for as many fathers as possible to go more deeply into the problem. I hope something will come of it.

I look forward to seeing you soon,

With warmest greetings in Christ,

Franjo Šeper

In May Rahner attempted to get an audience with John XXIII over the diaconate. He wrote:

I will ask König and Bea to take part in the audience. Of course I don't yet know whether they can. Indeed we don't even know whether the present Pope will be alive then. It seems to be uncertain.

I still can't see whether and when the passage on the diaconate in ch.2 of *De Ecclesia* will get through. They've begun with ch.3, but they now don't know when *that* will go forward, because other things are now thought to be more urgent. But the text on the diaconate is in the schema; I don't think that it's been quietly deleted. So *perhaps* it would even be best if it were simply given to the bishops before the Council in printed form, even if there were a note that no *vote* had been taken on it in the commission. I'll keep the matter in mind and sound out Tromp.

Rome, 20 May 1963

I've spoken to Tromp. The passage on the diaconate will not be voted on in the commission. It will appear in the schema and it will be left to the Council itself whether it wants to keep it or delete it. I couldn't speak to König and Bea about the audience, but I will try not to forget. ()

Yesterday I crossed swords with Ottaviani again in the session. I said that the church should not act so 'triumphally' in the new schema, as if it had solutions for all modern problems in its pocket. He grumbled about that afterwards in the session. But apparently König liked what I said. He laughed, and spoke of toes being trodden on.

Everything goes on terribly slowly. I don't know whether I shall get away from here before Whitsun. I could go to the Athos jubilee; I've been invited by the Patriarch. Cologne Radio would pay my fare. But no one gives me time for it. The audience with the General is shifted to the beginning of next week. So I still don't know anything about Munich. Today I'm having lunch with Höfer. In eight days he's going to give a birthday meal for Bea to which Bea is going; I'm invited too. Good God, how complicated the world is!

Rome, 21 May 1963

The lifting of the preliminary censorship, the death of Pope John XXIII and the election of Paul VI

I've seen the newly printed schema of the first two chapters of *De Ecclesia*. The text on the diaconate is in it. Philips even said to me that the note that this section was not really voted on in the theological commission is absent. I shall insist that this passage is truly commended at the beginning of July, when I have to give a report at a conference of all the German and Austrian bishops on the dogmatic schemata and write an opinion from them for Rome.

I'm not getting to the General till tomorrow. I wonder how it will go? I'm not very hopeful. But I will argue strongly for Munich.

I've just heard that the Pope has received the last rites. I wonder whether the next Pope will really let the Council go on in the autumn?

Rome, 27 May 1963

I got back from Rome today. () Yesterday the General gave me permission without any difficulty to accept a call to Munich if one came. Now I'm impatient to see whether one does come. () One could also do some good in Rome; at least prevent some things. () Ottaviani came only very rarely, if at all, to the sessions. But he was represented by Browne, the Dominican cardinal. I've also seen Colombo again. What if his Lord and Master (Montini) were to become Pope?

Innsbruck, 29 May 1963

Yesterday I told the Provincial what the General had decided. In the course of this next week Simmel will make enquiries in Munich to see whether this professorship was provided for in the budget negotiations in the local government debate and whether it has gone through. Then we shall gradually be able to see how promising things are.[36] () Otherwise at present there really isn't any news. In the last three days I have written an article on 'bishops' conferences' at the request of *Stimmen der Zeit*. It's actually to appear in the July number. I don't think that it is any more stupid than what the canon lawyers have already written on the subject. Namely, virtually nothing.

Yesterday I sent a note about the Pope to Vienna for *Time* (very short) and wrote a rather longer obituary for the *Volksbote*. I hope that I haven't put in more flattery than is unavoidable on such occasions. And anyway, on the whole I found Giovanni XXIII a most sympathetic character. Especially as he interceded for me very nicely, as the General again told me last Tuesday. In fact the HO has completely retreated in the matter (over the censorship). The General alone will be appointing my censors, and he will appoint the usual ones. And if I come to Munich, it will be even easier there.

Innsbruck, 2 June 1963

Thus the letters about the censorship are dated on one Pentecost and those about its abolition are dated at the next (1963). And the last mention is connected with the name of John XXIII.

I also heard (to my sorrow!) in Munich yesterday that the chair in Munich will only be founded next year, so that at present neither I nor Thielicke can hope for a professorship, though next year it is virtually certain. And I had so hoped to get away from here soon.()

I've just got the Ecclesia schema from Döpfner (the first two chapters). The diaconate business is in it. But I've not yet got down to an article for *Stimmen* on it.

Innsbruck, 8 June 1963

There's one anecdote about Giovanni and me that I can't really tell. I just know that in a conversation in the garden at Castelgandolfo he twice told O'Connell of the Papal observatory that Rahner seemed to be a very sound man and that they ought to leave him in peace (the Holy Office); the Jesuit General was responsible for such censorship and was man enough. () I don't know whether the story about Ottaviani and the Pope differing over me[37] is true. But the *Time* man in Rome tells me that it really is. () I don't know whether I can get down to work. In ten days I have to be ready with the opinion for the German and Austrian bishops (if I'm also to send it to Ratzinger and so on), and haven't even begun. But I've only just got the texts. () Please go to Harling[38] and settle with him whether the little lexicon can now appear in Italian. We can in fact wait until the new Pope is elected. But I personally think that this translation can now be risked, provided that it's done properly.

Innsbruck, 9 June 1963

I think that we can do the little lexicon in Italian under the new Pope. Indeed through Colombo I have a line to the supreme authority.

Today I got a letter from Max Müller.[39] Things are not as bad as I heard from Simmel. On the contrary. The professorship is approved. The faculty is officially requested to make a short list of three. It's quite certain that the choice will be made during this semester. Even if the ministry announces the call this year, it has money for it from another fund if the normal budgetary cover can only be provided next year. There could just be some delay, as (because) the parallel Protestant chair has not got so far. So things could drag out until the endof this year. *Haec de his.* ()

I hope that all goes well with the new Pope. Jungmann already knows him personally. I have the line through Colombo. And so I'm somewhat reassured, though of course the question remains whether and how far he can get beyond his diplomatic shadow and his hesitations.

Innsbruck, 22 June 1963

The continuation of work for the Council and the second period

Immediately after his accession to office, Paul VI had announced that the Council would continue, and despite the change of Pope, for Karl Rahner the work of giving opinions went on almost without a break.He was always particularly concerned about the theme of the diaconate.

I've just leafed through the schemata that König sent me the day before yesterday. The Ecclesia schema seems to be new yet again and printed differently. But the text on the diaconate is still in it and unchanged. Nor is there anything in it about this passage having been accepted without a vote by the commission. And to my surprise in p.26 n.37 our book on the diaconate is cited – the only modern work. So now your name, too, is in an official Council text. Ha ha! In the same note there is also a reference to the text in Ehses *CT* VI, 601, from the Council of Trent, to which the present diaconate people attach a good deal of importance. Tell that to Hannes Kramer, too. I have a bad conscience because I did not do the article for *Stimmen*. But I had no time for it. I think we've done what we could for this matter. Unfortunately there is no longer a separate schema for the diaconate. But if this text, which is fourteen lines long in the schema, remains, the door is open and in the long run we shall certainly get further. The notes on this text are almost half a page long and the matter is also discuuassed again in the accompanying commentary which is printed in the same schema. Philips has done that well. For if I myself (along with others) can do anything for the texts, Philips has advanced matters very considerably by leaving the text in the official version and adding nice notes. It's also thanks to him that both of us are quoted. I said nothing about it.[40]

Innsbruck, 23 June 1963

Rahner had to write opinions on the themes of the church, Mary (*De BMV*) and revelation, and in addition at the beginning of September had to work in Malines on a new text on the church in the modern world.

Today I've sent my bishops' opinions on the three dogmatic schemata of the Council to Döpfner for duplication. () I'm so tired.

Saarbrücken, 4 July 1963

Max Müller has given me more details about the Munich business. The real discussion in the faculty is on the 17th and then in the Senate on the 24th (of this month). The commission has unanimously put me well ahead in first place. Max thinks that all will go smoothly.

Saarbrücken, 11 July 1963

I'm in Terme Apollinari di Vicarello (but the address is the Germanicum). On 9 September I gave my lecture in Rome and got here on the 11th. This house belongs to the Germanicum, is at Lago di Bracciano, and is looked after by sisters; there have been baths (thermal springs in the house) since the time of the Etruscans. However, I'm not taking a cure here, but Exercises. I've still heard nothing from Munich, although Döpfner promised me that he would speed things up and let me know. If I hear nothing, I shall stay on here after the Exercises or go to Rome until the Council begins again. () I prepared the three opinions in Munich. The one against the present schema *De BMV* has come out very powerful. The two days in Malines (without Suenens himself) were very interesting, but strenuous. On one occasion I had to work till one in the morning; something that you may usually do, but I don't. I've lots of additional work with me, so

I've enough to do, even if I don't get back to Germany before the Council.

Terme, 12 September 1963

The Exercises will be finished on the evening of the day after tomorrow. Soon after that I shall go back to Rome. Döpfner will heave into sight on the 25th. There will be some things to do in connection with his new status at the Council.[41]

Terme, 17 September 1963

Döpfner is coming on Wednesday. After that I shall be back again in Rome. Today Philips sent me the schema *De activa praesentia Ecclesiae in mundo aedificando* which was cooked up by him and colleagues after our Malines discussion. But I haven't read it yet. I've still heard nothing from Munich. () In the last few days I've written about eighty pages (manuscript), partly incidental and partly substantial with some tricky points on themes in moral theology.[42] Of course there's no one who can type it out for me. () The Pope's speech on the reform of the Curia is clear. Perhaps at the Council there will now emerge a beginning of the beginnings of something practical. At least we can hope so.

Terme, 23 September 1963

Döpfner told me that the new Pope spoke very well of me. Where and how I didn't ask. I only said that in that case I can get back to work again. Which apparently didn't please him. For he said that Küng's speeches on his American trip were a great credit to him, here and not only with the Holy Office. () I haven't really heard anything here yet. Semmelroth is also here. Mörsdorf is coming and will be staying here in the house. Hirschmann (the boy Jesus in the temple, who can answer all the questions) gave his first new press conference yesterday. Of course I wasn't there. Kötting again made me an urgent offer of the dogmatics chair at Münster. I wrote to him that it is impracticable at present since I am almost promised for Munich and Rome would not be keen on Münster either, since the General has already said no to Münster once.

Rome, 27 September 1963

I must go straight back to St Peter's. But I don't plan to go every morning, even for the schema *De Ecclesia*. You waste so much time that way, if you have to go at 8.30 and aren't back home again until 1. And you can't do anything else there, since the tribune on which we sit is so narrow. Yesterday it was said that no new *periti* are going to be nominated.

Rome, 1 October 1963

Tell Hannes Kramer that today Döpfner will be speaking in the Council on the passage in the schema on the church about the diaconate. He will defend it really energetically along with the sentence that celibacy is not necessary for it. On Friday the passage was vigorously attacked by three people in the Aula. To that degree it is very good that Döpfner is springing into the breach. I wrote the text for him yesterday and of course he changed some things round, but didn't alter any of the content. That was my satisfaction yesterday. Lunch with Leiprecht,[43] with whom I have to go to a session of the commission today because they aren't letting Wulf in, poor man, because he's not a *peritus*. On Saturday morning I did a text with the help of Semmelroth, Pfister and Ratzinger on the collegiality of the episcopate (against Ruffini, who vigorously attacked it on Friday). On Saturday afternoon in Frings' office I went through the whole galley proof and checked it. On Sunday, i.e. yesterday, the four Latin pages were then distributed through all available channels. We produced 2400 copies in this way and got them out. I hope that it's some use. It's terrible how hard one has to fight to make the slightest progress. On Friday I spent a whole morning with Küng, preparing a passage in a speech to the Council for Rusch[46] (I don't go into the *aula*, that takes too much time) so that the local communities can have some rights at the altar and not just the bishops. – I've just spoken to Rusch again. He's passed the matter on to the suffragan bishop of Fulda, so that he can speak on it. For today Rusch has to speak on collegiality in scripture and needs the the whole ten minutes. We must divide the themes in this way and thus toss the ball from side to side. On Thursday I and Mörsdorf (I think he was very pleased) together did a text for the Aula and made some suggestions for improving the schema text on the relationship between the two *potestates* and the three *munera* in the ministry of the church, a story on which the sun seems to rise and set for Mörsdorf. Höffner has undertaken to introduce that. There was also a session of the faith commission last week. I've already given a press conference, some of which is to be on television. I don't know when. Yesterday I gave a television interview for America for the 'Catholic Hour'. They say that it goes out from over a hundred stations. The day before yesterday I brought Döpfner a protest from a group of bishops and *periti* that they don't want Maximus to speak unless he speaks Latin. This afternoon the French bishops want to make a joint protest against that (the story about the objections is already in the newspapers). Döpfner knew nothing about it. Felici must have done it off his own bat. It will be interesting to see what happens next. This afternoon Wulf is coming to me to prepare for this afternoon's session of the commission on the religious, i.e. so that I know what I'm to do for it. I'm telling you that only so that you can see that I'm not completely without work. In October I also have to write a piece for the Protestant pastor Finke and Abbot Klein (Frankfurt or Trier) for their joint book on ministry. Yes, I would be glad to be finished here. The liturgists are proud of their schema. But will anything really come out of it? And in the end won't it all be just the same: little well-meant improvements which don't change much. Still nothing from Munich.

Rome, 7 October 1963

When Rahner says that he doesn't go to the sessions, he means the gatherings of bishops in St Peter's, not the sessions of the commissions. The letters of 27 and 30 October touch on the important question of the vote on whether the text on Mary should be included in that on the church, which is what Rahner had fought for, or not.

I've still heard nothing from Munich. – I've nothing new to report about the Council. I don't go there. All in all I've been there only for two sessions. In the morning I and Wulf have to do something else for Döpfner. There were speeches for and against the diaconate in the sessions. I think that at all events the position is that later bishops' conferences can have it if they want to, from the Pope. I hope that we shall also get it into the schema, or rather, keep it there. Today Döpfner was raging mad at a Yugoslavian bishop who among other things spoke against it. () I myself am rather lazy; one should do more here behind the scenes at the

Council. Tomorrow afternoon I have to be with the German observers and inform them about the schema and the Pope's speech. Tomorrow night I'm giving a lecture to South American bishops. A cardinal there has read 'Primacy and Episcopacy' with interest.

Rome, 9 October 1963

There's a good deal to tell about the Council. It drags wearily on. I really have a lot of work. For example tomorrow morning another session of the theological commission and in the evening the Brazilian bishops. This morning Küng is coming so that we can do something for Suenens. What he said recently was cooked up by Küng with a little help from me in my rooms here. The vote is on Tuesday as to whether Mariology is to be put back in the schema on the church. If König doesn't win on this vote, having argued our case, I'm to blame, since I've more or less set it out for him. You will have heard that last Monday Ottaviani attacked us (Martelet, Ratzinger and myself) as purveyors of texts which disturbed the fathers. He didn't mention our names in the *aula*. But everyone knows who is meant, and the Italian press is also said to have given the names. Yesterday evening, though, a great many theologians came to the *Sacramentum mundi* reception, and Colombo has done its cause good as a result, simply because he is a friend of the Pope. I'm also attacked again in a Roman journal (which I haven't seen) because in the French *Mission and Grace* I make it too easy for people in heaven. 'In that case, what's mission for?', they ask. In the last session of the theological commission I also had to have a vigorous go at a bishop in defence of the diaconate, although the theme was not actually on the agenda. I don't know how that will turn out. Bidagor spoke to me very nicely at the reception yesterday. He said that I was the first before the Council to have given an opinion for the Council; they could have made a good schema out of it, but unfortunately it got dropped again. However, it really had taken into account everything that was now being discussed.

Rome, 27 October 1963

I'm content with yesterday's vote, because I was afraid that the others would get the majority. They put out vast propaganda. A Ukrainian bishop distributed pamphlets in front of the Aula, the Spaniards distributed printed leaflets everywhere, Roschini produced a brochure, speaking of a fight for and against the Madonna: Balic distributed a long brochure printed on the Vatican press like a schema. He will not understand that one cannot do otherwise in such a question of procedure. The Pope wants the schema *De libertate religiosa* produced by the Bea commission to come soon. Then there will probably be more rows. Today there is a vote on the basic questions concerned with further work on the schema on the church. How will it turn out? Particularly in view of the diaconate? The seven sub-commissions of the faith commission are now getting to work, very slowly. The Pope has told Ottaviani to work more quickly, which is very painful for him. They're dawdling along and working carefully because they don't want the thing. But because the sub-commissions are so formed that the *periti* have to do the work in them, there will be yet more vexation at the Most Holy. For in that case even the free time will go.

I've still heard nothing from Munich. Before long Maunz[45] or at least Höfer, who has written to Munich about things, ought to reply.

Rome, 30 October 1963

The attacks on Rahner did not stop. But despite many appeals to the church government to intervene, from now on they no longer led to administative measures against him. In the work for the sub-commission the main topic was the theme of the collegiality of bishops and their relationship to the Pope.

I hope that I shall begin lectures in Munich in the summer semester, and not lecture in Innsbruck before that. () I've been vigorously attacked in a long article in an international missionary journal *Le Christ au monde*. At the end questions are put to the fathers of the Council. The same thing in another Italian journal. The work here is getting steadily worse. From now on we shall probably have a sub-commission session of the theological commission every day. Nothing today. Still no news from Munich. Evidently Höfer's letter didn't do any good.

Rome, 6 November 1963

Dead tired after the session of the theological commission in which Ottaviani again lost a vote 18:5 (he wanted to torpedo the Bea text on religious freedom). I want to reply very quickly with many thanks for your letter. () Otherwise no news. At least nothing occurs to my poor head. This week has been the worst sweat in the whole of the Council for me. I don't know whether I shall be able to produce the *relatio* which had to be ready this week. The other three *periti* on my sub-commission who are working on it are either against me (Salaverri, Maccarone) or somewhat lame (Ratzinger).

Rome, 11 November 1963

I've got flu, so perhaps I shall go straight back to bed, though it's morning. () Excuse me for writing so little. I've now completely finished my *relatio*. Now it must be typed.

Rome, 19 November 1963

This evening I'm going to Naples for Sunday to give two lectures to the Jesuit scholastics and *patres* there. Before that I want to send you warmest greetings. Another week past. Yesterday I prepared the joint text of our *relatio* with Ratzinger, Maccarone and Salaverri (with remarks in it that we are not agreed on important points). I gave the special text that Ratzinger and I wrote to Philips two days ago. I'm anxious to see how things go when we present our views and counter-views to the four bishops (including Parente) of our sub-commission and whether we get anywhere over the question of collegiality in this session of the Council during the full session of the theological commission. Moreover, soon some members will be added to this commission, including a vice-president and a second secretary. I'm eager to see what comes out of that. () Still no letter from Munich. Another good week, and then we shall be finished here. Next week I have lectures almost every evening in addition to the sessions of the commission: to the Belgians, the French, the Jesuits, the people from the Propaganda school, the Brazilian bishops. How glad I shall be to get away from here! How slowly the wheels continue to move! I think that I won't get the letter from Munich as long as I'm here, so I shall then go straight to Munich and only go back to Innsbruck when I have to prepare for the move. I hope that's how it works out. () On Monday I have to go with Kälin, Schmaus, Volk, Meurers and Ludwig to the Pope for this Institute of the

Görresgesellschaft. () Scherer wrote that the little lexicon will also be translated into English. How do things stand with the Dutch and French translations? And the Italian? – In a pastoral letter from Bishop Carli of Segni to his clergy (which consist of 16 parishes and twenty-nine secular clergy, so that the bishop certainly has time to write sixty-page pastoral letters to his clergy) I am also cited as an example of how people today depart from traditional language. () You will have heard the good story that someone wrote on the Mercedes of a Council father: *receperunt mercedem suam* (Matt.6.5). It's a good thing that neither of us has a Mercedes.

Rome, 23 November 1963

The call to Munich, progress in work for the Council and the beginning of activities in Munich

On 22 November 1963 the Philosophical Faculty in Munich was finally told that the call had gone out from the ministry to Karl Rahner. On hearing this news Rahner wrote:

I haven't yet got the letter from Munich. But I think that it will really come at last. So I have good reason for going to Munich first from here at the end of next week. And then immediately pack and be off from Innsbruck. () Yesterday I had a big fight with Salaverri in a session of the sub-committee. He was blazing angry when I quoted from his own book to demonstrate that what he says there is what he is now fighting against: collegiality. But I think that we shall battle through the most important things. Grillmeier, who is on the diaconate sub-commission, said that there is good hope that we can hold the pass so far.

Rome, 29 November 1963

Today is the last day here. Tomorrow I fly to Munich. () So at least to begin with I shall be in Veterinärstrasse, Munich. If it is possible on the ministry side, I hope to have completed the negotiations about the post before Christmas, now that D. brought the official call letter on 2 December; then I shall pack in Innsbruck and move. Then I shall be in Munich.

Rome, 5 December 1963

Today I've heard that I have to be in Rome for sessions of the commission from 19 to 26 January. Similarly it is virtually certain that I have to be in Rome on 2 March. I can't imagine that the sessions of the full theological commission will be able to end so quickly (in January it's only a sub-commission) that I can be in Freiburg on 5 March.[46]

Munich, 27 December 1963

There's a lot of work here. Yesterday we spent the day in the HO, where otherwise only the HO cardinals have their sessions. We were quite alone, and not even the *consultores* were there, but only Parente the assessor. So we sat down and talked cheerfully.

Rome, 23 January 1964

Not much news here. The sessions of the fifth sub-commission were finished on Saturday, peacefully and without excitement. Parente continued to be reasonable and friendly. Felici expressed a wish to get to know me. I wonder what he wants? () I don't know how long the sessions of the religious commission will last; they begin again today after a preliminary session on Friday. We may come to blows then, since it is a quite sinister group.

Rome, 27 January 1964

From many letters which report an enormous pressure of work and deadlines, a situation which was not made any easier by the new beginning in Munich, I simply quote one:

I'm sitting here and feel desperate. I just can't cope with any more work. I wrote a new article for Simmel, for *Stimmen*. Since Wednesday I've been sitting at an opinion from Rome. I've also desperately read proofs for *LTK*. New ones are coming today though I haven't finished the old ones. Now I have to do an outline text for Rome. And when will I be able to prepare my lectures for Munich? Constant visits. There is also a mountain of unread manuscripts from *Sacramentum Mundi*. Heinz[47] has also written, about *Concilium*. And so it goes on.

Munich, 28 March 1964

Yesterday afternoon and tomorrow I have to fight again on the relationship between scripture and tradition. But at least Schauf has not come. However, Florit of Florence is more obstinate than before. They are saying that there is going to have to be a fourth period of the Council. Terrible. But unfortunately even I can't see how they could do things faster. Yet a longer period does not guarantee that things will be any better.

Rome, 21 April 1964

I got back from Rome yesterday. tired. But one can always see to it there that the worst does not happen and that small points of contact are put in the schemata for a later theology. That's not much, yet it's a great deal.

Munich, 27 April 1964

Rahner did not change this view of the Council over the next twenty years; at that time the Council was not yet half-way through.

The following texts speak of the first beginnings of Foundations, *which originally came into being as the first lectures for Munich.*

I still have so much post; I've looked through the proofs very quickly and accurately, as before, and above all I've dictated my lectures like a madman. I've already 120 forty-line pages. That's a good beginning, but only a beginning. What I'm dictating doesn't seem to me to be so bad. But I very much wonder whether it's not too abstract and boring for the actual audience. However, in the end that doesn't matter. For the book that can come out of it is more important, even if it becomes more learned theology.

Munich, 5 May 1964

D. told me that my first lecture was boring (or something to that effect) because I read it out. Perhaps he's right. But I probably will not be able to decide to speak extempore because in that case everything will be too inaccurate and long-drawn-out. I'm rather bothered. Now I must write another opinion on the Mariology in the church schema for the German bishops. But I already have enough of the lectures in writing to last to the end of the semester.

Munich, 14 May 1964

At the moment I'm very hard pressed. I shall probably have no alternative but to be in Rome again from 1-7 June.
Munich, 20 June 1964

My lectures are thought to be too difficult. My God, what shall I do? I can't change them. And if I made them even cheaper, there would be nothing there. I could simplify things if I had more time and could explain every sentence I utter for a quarter of an hour or more. But I don't have time, unless I can lecture for ten semesters on the same theme. What shall I do? In the end I don't really care about the complaint. For if a reasonable book comes out of them, more service is done to the church than if I edify a few dumb people like Guardini. That's what I think. What about you?

Munich, 30 May 1964

In August 1964 Karl Rahner was in Freiburg. As he could telephone from Munich more easily than from Innsbruck, his comments on the Council in letters gradually came to an end. He no longer thought that he could make a significant contribution to the Council, and increasingly turned towards his theological plans:

Today I fly to Rome. I shall be in Feldafing from 25-30 September.

Munich, 30 May 1964

I still don't know how long I shall be in Rome. Certainly I shall be here on 24 October for the meeting of the *Concilium* people, as I have to speak on the same day at a conference in Rome of the Catholic Academy in Bavaria. But it's quite possible that on 15 October I shall fly to Munich, in order to be able to use the time until 24 October to prepare the lectures. () So far I haven't been in the *aula*, since for a good deal of the time schemata are being discussed which don't concern me. The work is moving on at a very brisk pace. Only the work of the theological commission is dragging rather. Above all, people are not very sure who is working it all out in *modi*. Here there may possibly be enough reason to be somewhat mistrustful and to keep a sharp eye on things. But as I've said, we shall see next Tuesday. By and large, however, there has been quite an inclination to finish things off, though officially there has been no statement now that it's coming to an end. I think that it's impossible for the commission work to be concluded in any reasonable way. The schema on revelation could do with some very significant improvements (inerrancy) in two or three places. Then it won't really be *too* bad. As far as I can see, the press accounts in *FAZ* and the *Süddeutsche Zeitung* are often crude or stupid. There can hardly be any more great sensations that are worth headlines. But the work is going well and the results of the votes are really amazingly good in many respects. I'm getting a bit sick of Schema 13 on the presence of the church in the modern world, because people have kept referring to this schema in rather too pretentious a way; but in reality it's fairly thin, and in its basic foundations it's theologically very thin. It makes no difference to me if I'm away for the discussion of this text because, given the present state of the text, from now on there is no way of saying what should be said. It is also questionable whether here the Council can in fact say what needs to be said. A larger commission of very wise and experienced people would have to work that out over a longish period.

Rome, 8 October 1964

The two tiny notes from the fourth period of the Council read as though Karl Rahner no longer felt very involved in the Council:

The best thing here is the fine weather. Otherwise not much is happening.

Rome, 30 September 1965

The Council is tedious.

Rome, 18 October 1965

However, he has continually indicated what he thought of the Council as a whole in his Schriften, *right down to the last volume: it was a good and great event and produced at least the 'beginning of beginnings' of a way forwards and not backwards.*

Notes

1. J.B.Metz, *Unterbrechungen. Theologisch-politische Perspektiven und Profile*, Gütersloh 1981, which include 'Karl Rahner — ein theologisches Leben', (43-57) 56.
2. *Not und Segen des Gebetes*, Freiburg im Breisgau 1977, 127. Rahner regarded this as an important book: *Karl Rahner im Gespräch* (henceforth = *Gespräch*), ed. P.Imhof and H.Biallowons, 2 vols, Munich 1982, 1983, II, 57. An English translation is in preparation.
3. *Glaube, der die Erde liebt*, Freiburg im Breisgau 1966, 158.
4. *Not und Segen*, 66f.
5. Ibid., 12f.
6. Ibid., 18.
7. J.B.Metz, *Den Glauben lernen und lehren. Dank an Karl Rahner*, Munich 1984, 25.
8. Rahner, *Theological Investigations* 7, 45.
9. Rahner, *Gebete des Lebens*, Freiburg im Breisgau 1984, 179f.
10. In the Preface to *Theological Investigations* 5.
11. *Gebete*, 143.
12. Ibid.
13. Ibid., 141f.
14. From *Schriften zur Theologie* XV, 374f.
15. As he says with Ignatius of Loyola, ibid., 374.
16. *Theological Investigations* 11, 157-9.
17. J.B.Metz, *Glauben lernen*, 23, 21f.
18. Rahner, *Theological Investigations* 6, 247.
19. *Schriften* XV, 407.
20. *Gespräch* II, 150.
21. Some have also been included in his lesser writings published by the Verlag ars sacra, Munich. To be added to them are also meditations like those on everyday things, those on the church's year or those in the pocket book *Glaube, der die Erde liebt*.
22. Karl Rahner, *Spiritual Exercises*, Sheed and Ward 1967, 8. Rahner's book *Meditations on Priestly Life*, Sheed and Ward 1975, also comes from lectures on the *Exercises*. Karl Rahner lectured on them fifty times between 1934 and 1984.
23. *Schriften* XV, 376.
24. See n.22.
25. This interview appears in *Gespräch* II, 31-41; the quotation comes

from p. 34. For Rahner's own experience of the exercises see ibid., 51. He also discusses them in *Karl Rahner, Bekenntnisse*, ed. G.Sporschill, Vienna and Munich 1984, 57f. (henceforth = *Bekenntnisse*).

26. K.H.Neufeld, 'Unter Brüdern. Zur Frühgeschichte der Theologie K.Rahners aus der Zusammenarbeit mit H.Rahner', in *Wagnis Theologie*, ed. H.Vorgrimler, Freiburg im Breisgau 1979, 341-54.

27. In both the publications mentioned above in nn.1, 7: *Glauben lernen*, 14, *Unterbrechungen*, 44.

28. *Unterbrechungen*, 46.

29. Ibid., 45.

30. *Gespräch* II, 166.

31. Ibid., I, 40f.

32. J.B.Metz, *Unterbrechungen*, 48.

33. Ibid., 49.

34. W.Pannenberg, 'Befreiung zur Unbefangenheit des Denkens', in *Bekenntnisse*, (67-77) 67f.

35. J.B.Metz, *Unterbrechungen*, 49.

36. Ibid., 51.

37. H.Erharter and W.Zauner, 'Dank an Karl Rahner', *Diakonia* 15, 1984, (276ff.) 277.

38. From 'Anthropologie', *LTK* I, 1957, 624f.

39. For example in *Theological Investigations* 20, 10, 19. He commented on *Humanae Vitae* e.g. in *Theological Investigations* 11, 263-87. He accepted a doctoral thesis from Haye van der Meer on the ordination of women (published in 1969) which argued that the reasons against such ordination were theologically untenable.

40. F.K.Mayr, 'Vermutungen zur Karl Rahners Sprachstil', in *Wagnis Theologie* (see n.26), (143-59) 148. The German sentence, modelled on Rahner's style, uses an enormous number of participles which cannot adequately be reproduced in English.

41. E.g. in Karl Rahner, *Bekenntnisse*, 36-43.

42. G.Sporschill, in *Bekenntnisse*, 82.

43. I would like to mention the particularly fine obituary in *Der Spiegel* of 9 April 1984.

44. A.Görres, 'Nothelfer fur Leib und Seele', *Süddeutsche Zeitung* of 5 March 1984, 22.

45. *Bekenntnisse*, 49f.

46. The speech is in *Schriften* XV, 373-408. The term spiritual testament comes in *Bekenntnisse*, 58.

47. Comments in Karl Rahner, *I Remember, An autobiographical interview with Meinold Krauss*, Crossroad Publishing Company and SCM Press 1985, 63.

48. Karl Rahner, *Bekenntnisse*, 25.

49. The dismissal of the Jesuit General Pedro Arrupe by John Paul II on 5 October 1981 affected Rahner more deeply than he indicated in *Gespräch* II, 273. At that time he telephoned me late at night, which was not usually his custom; he was shaken and upset. Fr Kolvenbach, the new General, wrote him a particularly fine letter for his eightieth birthday.

50. *Schriften* XV, 380.
51. Ibid., 380f.
52. Ibid., 386f.
53. The last three quotations, ibid., 192f.
54. *Unterbrechungen*, 55.
55. Ibid.
56. On John XXIII, *Gespräch* II, 26; also *Bekenntnisse*, 33; *I Remember*, 86f. On Paul VI *Gespräch* II, 26f.; also ibid., 217; *I Remember*, 88f. On John Paul II *Bekenntnisse*, 47; also *I Remember*, 12f., 94ff.
57. *Gespräch* II, 147; cf. *I Remember*, 32.
58. H.Erharter and W.Zauer, op.cit. (see n.37), 278.
59. *Bekenntnisse*, 56.
60. Reprinted in *Bekenntnisse*, 61-5.
61. *Gespräch* II, 49 (by mistake it has Paul Gogarten there).
62. Ibid., 50.
63. *Bekenntnisse*, 58.
64. Ibid., she lived from 1875 to 1976, his father Karl from 1868 to 1934. Both are buried in the cemetery at Freiburg-Günterstal.
65. *I Remember*, 24f.
66. *Gespräch* II, 147.
67. Ibid., 148.
68. In *I Remember*, 52-4.
69. *Bekenntnisse*, 15f.; cf. *I Remember*, 22ff.
70. *Bekenntnisse*, 14.
71. Ibid.
72. *I Remember*, 33f.
73. *Gespräch* II, 48.
74. *I Remember*, 23.
75. *I Remember*, 36.
76. Ibid., 24.
77. *Bekenntnisse*, 49.
78. *Gespräch* I, 32, here Rahner also mentions Maréchal's main work; also *Gespräch* II, 50, 149.
79. Neufeld, op.cit. (see n.26), 348.
80. *I Remember*, 39f.
81. Neufeld, op.cit., 345.
82. Already in 1930, Neufeld, op.cit., 342.
83. Ibid., 345.
84. Cf.e.g. his observations in *Gespräch* II, 153; *I Remember*, 56f.
85. Neufeld, op.cit., 343ff.
86. *Gespräch* II, 51. Cf. Karl Rahner, *Theological Investigations* 16, 130ff., on interpretations of Ignatius.
87. *I Remember*, 44.
88. Ibid., 45,47. Cf. also *Gespräch* I, 31f.; II, 50, 151f.
89. *Geist in Welt*, Innsbruck 1939, 407.
90. Ibid., 13f.
91. *I Remember*, 43.
92. *Hörer des Wortes*, Munich 1941, 203.
93. Ibid., 203.
94. Ibid., 209.
95. For the relationship between the two brothers, H.Rahner, 'Eucharist-icon fraternitatis', *Gott in Welt* II, Freiburg 1964, 895-9, is important.

96. For the whole process see K.H.Neufeld, op.cit. (see n.26), 349-52.

97. Ibid., 351.

98. Rahner, *Theological Investigations* 1, 7.

99. K.H.Neufeld, op.cit., 352ff.

100. See T.Mass-Ewand, *Die Krise der Liturgischen Bewegung in Deutschland und Österreich*, Regensburg 1981. The Gröber memorandum is reprinted on pp.259-85.

101. An extract is printed in T.Mass-Ewand, op.cit., 599-608. He discusses the attitude of the Austrian bishops, ibid., 304-38.

102. Cf. the introduction to the *Rahner-Register*, Zurich 1974, an aid to research produced by K.H.Neufeld.

103. *Concilium* 19, 1983, 820. E.Schillebeeckx tells the story of the origin of *Concilium* from the first discussions in 1958, in conversation with H.Oosterhuis and P.Hoogeven, in *God is New Each Moment*, T.&.T.Clark and Seabury Press 1983, 75.

104. He gives examples in *Bekenntnisse*, 22ff.

105. Ibid., 21f.

106. *Gespräch* II, 217. Pius XII's comments appear in *AAS* 46, 1954, 668-70.

107. *AAS* 53, 1961, 236; *LTK* supplement, *Das Zweite Vatikanische Konzil* I, 256.

108. For details see the appendix, 'Karl Rahner: A Brief Correspondence from the Time of the Council'.

109. *Bekenntnisse*, 26.

110. There is a summary by G.Caprile in *LTK* supplement, *Das Zweite Vatikanische Konzil* III, 697.

111. Cf.Y.Congar, 'Erinnerungen an eine Episode auf dem II.Vatikanischen Konzil'. Appendix, Zwei Schema-Entwürfe *De revelatione Dei*, I. Karl Rahner unter Mitwirkung von Joseph Ratzinger, *Glaube im Prozess*, ed. E.Klinger and K.Wittstadt, Freiburg im Breisgau 1984, 32-50.

112. *Bekenntnisse*, 27.

113. Cf. H.Vorgrimler, 'Busse und Krankensalbung', *Handbuch der Dogmengeschichte* IV/3, Freiburg im Breisgau 1978, 214.

114. K.H.Neufeld, 'Theologen und Konzil', *Stimmen der Zeit* 109, 1984, (156-66) 161.

115. Cf. K.Rahner, *Gnade als Freiheit*, Freiburg im Breisgau 1968, 253-65; the evaluation of Guardini on his eightieth birthday, *I Remember*, 73f.

116. *I Remember*, 75.

117. *Gespräch*, I, 65f.

118. *Theological Investigations* 11, 263ff.

119. *I Remember*, 83.

120. Cf. the collection edited by K.Rahner, *Zum Problem Unfehlbarkeit*, Freiburg im Breisgau 1971, with several contributions by Rahner.

121. *Gespräch* II, 226ff.

122. Kuno Füssel has collected the most important articles by Rahner on the theology of the future in the paperback *K.Rahner, Theologie der Zukunft*, Munich 1971.

123. *Kritisches Wort*, Freiburg im Breisgau 1970, 233.

124. *Schriften* XV, 141. For the dialogues of the Paulusgesellschaft and the *Internationale Dialog-Zeitschrift* cf. also *Gespräch* II, 156f. (my name becomes Furtwängler there).

125. Some comments on this are collected in *Kritisches Wort* (see n.123).

126. *Einigung der Kirchen*, 112.

127. P.Lapide and K.Rahner, *Heil von den Juden?*, Mainz 1983.

128. *Theologisches* no.28, Abensberg 1972, 540, 542.

129. Cf. Rahner's arguments in his articles on the *magisterium*, dogmatic statements and the problem of infallibilty (see also n.120).

130. *Kritisches Wort*, 27. Rahner composed a fine *Laudatio* for Balthasar's sixtieth brithday in 1965 which was reprinted in many papers.

131. For Rahner's soteriology see *Theodramatik* III, Einsiedeln 1980, 253-62.

132. *Gespräch* II, 245f.

133. *Theological Investigations* 13, 127.

134. *Gespräch* II, 46f.

135. J.B.Metz, *Glaube in Geschichte und Gesellschaft*, Mainz 1977, section 9, especially 143ff.

136. H.Vorgrimler (ed.), *Wagnis Theologie*, Freiburg im Breisgau 1979, 258.

137. K.Rahner, 'Erfahrungen eines Katholischen Theologen', in *Vor dem Geheimnis Gottes den Menschen verstehen*, ed. K.Lehmann, Munich 1984, (105-119) 119.

138. *Gespräch* II, 167f.

139. Ibid., 301.

140. *I Remember*, 111.

141. *Gespräch* I, 316.

142. Ibid., 299.

143. Ibid., II, 260.

144. K.Rahner, 'Laudatio auf Erich Przywara', *Gnade als Freiheit*, Freiburg im Breisgau 1968, 266-73, Balthasar's remark is on 271.

145. *Theological Investigations* 16, 244 n.1.

146. *Theological Investigations* 16, 238f.

147. *Theological Investigations* 18, 101.

148. *Theological Investigations* 20, 175f.

149. This article on old age was included in *Schriften* XV.

Appendix

1. The texts of the letters of 11 February 1963, 20 May 1964, 30 May 1964, 8 September 1964, 30 September 1964, 8 October 1964, 30 September 1965 and 18 October 1965 are published here for the first time. They were left out of *Orientierung* because of their length.

2. At the time O.Simmel SJ was editor of *Stimmen der Zeit*. The reference is to the article by K.Rahner, 'Zur Theologie des Konzils', in *Stimmen der Zeit* 169, 1962, 321-39.

3. Namely K.Rahner, 'Die Theologie der Erneuerung des Diakonats', in *Diaconia in Christo*, ed. K.Rahner and H.Vorgrimler, Freiburg im Breisgau

1962, 285-324. The Roman opinion is Rahner's text of 1961 for the commission on the sacraments.

4. A helpful contact in Rome was our fellow Alemannian Burkhard Schneider SJ, church historian at the Gregorian Papal University.

5. Dr Robert Scherer, at that time the chief theological reader at Herder Verlag, was responsible for the foreign translations of the *Concise Theological Dictionary*.

6. Hermann Schäufele, from 1958 to 1977 Archbishop of Freiburg im Breisgau, was protector of the *Lexikon für Theologie und Kirche*.

7. A reference to the manuscript of a book by Küng on the Council.

8. Rahner knew that he would see Cardinal König at the Austrian Catholics' Day in Salzburg, at which Rahner gave his famous theological speech 'Do not Stifle the Spirit'.

9. Rahner had been invited to a small Teilhard symposium at Whitsun 1962 in Venice to which I was also to go.

10. E.Schillebeeckx OP, Flemish professor of theology in Nijmegen, a friend of Rahner's; M.F.J.Marlet SJ, Dutch professor of philosophy in Amsterdam and at the time in Innsbruck; Cardinal Alfrink, Archbishop of Utrecht, a towering figure at the Second Vatican Council.

11. Hermann Volk, consecrated Bishop of Mainz that week, a friend and former colleague of Rahner's in dogmatics; Josef Höfer, prelate and legate at the Vatican Embassy to West Germany, and with Rahner editor of the *Lexikon für Theologie und Kirche*.

12. Rahner then wrote on 26 June 1962: 'The matter need no longer be kept secret.'

13. Petrus van Gestel SJ (1897-1972) was assistant for the German speaking provinces at the office of the Jesuit General in Rome under P.Janssens (i.e. until 1965).

14. At that time I was preparing for the Flemish publisher Lannoo in Tielt, with Rahner's help, a short book about Karl Rahner's life, thought and work. This appeared in 1962 in Flemish and later in other languages; during the Council it was some help in introducing Rahner to foreign bishops and theologians.

15. *Veterum sapientia*, a constitution of John XXIII dated 1962, which emphasized Latin as a church language. Cardinal Alfredo Ottaviani, prefect of the Holy Office, was responsible for the preliminary censorship.

16. I am keeping Rahner's abbreviation HO for the Holy Office in Rome.

17. J.N.Schasching SJ was Provincial of the Austrian Jesuit province from July 1961. E.Coreth SJ was Rector of the Jesuit college in Innsbruck from August 1961; the two were Karl Rahner's immediate 'superiors'.

18. H.Krone was a cabinet minister under K.Adenauer.

19. H.de Lubac SJ, Y.Congar OP, M.D.Chenu OP, all well-known theologians of the renewal movement in France; S.Lyonnet SJ and M.Zerwick SJ, professors at the Pontifical Biblical Institute in Rome; J.Fuchs SJ, moral theologian at the Gregorian in Rome. Church 'measures' against the first three already began in the time of Pius XII and lasted until the Council; the Biblical Institute was censured in the time of John XXIII and the professors mentioned were disciplined.

20. Dr Oscar Bettschart, at that time theological reader at Benzinger Verlag, which was then in Ensiedeln.

21. Rahner later expressed his gratitude to this group, among other things by dedicating *Schriften* V to them. When Adenauer's doctor Martini told him what was happening, he joined in this plea for Karl Rahner through diplomatic channels.

22. Prof. Dr Paul Martini of the University of Bonn, doctor to Chancellor Adenauer and member of the Paulusgesellschaft.

23. Karl Rahner spoke at the German Catholics' Day about 'The Faith of the Priest Today'. The invitation to this held despite the preliminary censorship.

24. Augustine Bea SJ, Old Testament scholar, influential adviser to Pius XII, nominated cardinal by John XXIII, a cautious tactitian until the end of the Council, when he showed marked courage.

25. The reference is the outline on the *depositum fidei*, the deposit of faith.

26. Herbert Schauf, dogmatic theologian in Aachen, defender of the 'two sources' of divine revelation. Cf. his contribution in the Festschrift for Rahner, *Glaube im Prozess*, Freiburg im Breisgau 1984, 66-98.

27. Sebastian Tromp SJ, dogmatic theologian at the Gregorian; Frans Hürth SJ, moral theologian at the Gregorian; influential Roman theologians, *consultores* (advisers) to the so-called Holy Office, both being crucially involved in the Roman outlines for the Council.

28. K.Rahner, 'Über das Latein als Kirchensprache', *ZKT* 84, 1962, 257-99. The article did not have to go through the provisional censorship because at the time of this measure it was already at the printer and had passed the normal censorship. A *miramur* is a church rebuke, named after the opening word, 'We are amazed'.

29. Archbishop P.Parente, as assessor of the so-called Holy Office a very close collaborator with Cardinal Ottaviani.

30. Gérard Philips (1899-1972), Belgian dogmatic theologian, a very important theologian at the Council, secretary of the theological commission, a key figure along with Bishop A.Charue of Namur.

31. It was directed against the outline on the two sources of divine revelation. Many of the Germans who helped vigorously with the duplication are now bishops, including Karl Lehmann, at that time a pupil of E Dhanis SJ, for whom he produced his theological dissertation at the Gregorian; he is now bishop of Mainz.

32. The reference is to the joint commission which was to be led by Cardinals Ottaviani and Bea. Cf. K.Rahner, *Bekenntnisse*, ed. G.Sporschill, Vienna 1984, 27f.; *LTK, Das Zweite Vatikanische Konzil* III, 633, 666. Joseph Schröffer was at that time Bishop of Euchstatt; he later became a cardinal in the Curia.

33. C.Balic OFM, Roman professor of theology, Mariologist.

34. At that time Ottaviani told Rahner that the preliminary censorship was only intended to protect him, Rahner, from friends who understood him wrongly. Rahner replied that this was a privilege which he would forego. Cf. K.Rahner, *Bekenntnisse*, 26.

35. Rahner is speaking here of the French translation of his book *Mission*

and Grace. It appeared in France in the form of a number of booklets and had a great following.

36. The process was long drawn out because in contrast to Guardini's time a parallel Protestant chair had to be established, for which they hoped to get Helmut Thielicke.

37. In its issue of 14 December 1962 *Time* magazine had reported that Ottaviani had asked the Pope to send Rahner back from the Council to Innsbruck (as being a theological nuisance); John XXIII was said to have refused this request. When I tried to include this information in the German edition of my Rahner biography the Munich Generalvicariate told me (reference 2015); 'The *imprimatur* will be given only on condition that the account in *Time* and the conclusions drawn in it are withdrawn. 13 April 1963, Matthias Defregger, Vicar General.'

38. Johannes Harling was at that time director of Herderbücherei. A qualified translator for the Italian edition was not found until 1968 because of the complicated task. Carlo Colombo, professor of dogmatics in Milan and a co-editor of *Sacramentum Mundi*, was a personal friend of Paul VI.

39. Professor Dr Max Müller, Director of Philosophical Seminary I at the University of Münster, backed Rahner's call to Munich. Like Rahner, he was a member of the Catholic Heidegger school.

40. In the final version of all the Council texts, all the references to the scholarly works on which a Council text was based were again deleted.

41. Cardinal Döpfner was nominated one of the four moderators of the Council on 14 September 1963 by Paul VI.

42. Rahner used this material (the background of which was, among other things, the problem of birth control) in the book by A.Röper, *Objektive und subjektive Moral. Ein Gespräch mit Karl Rahner*, Freiburg im Breisgau 1971.

43. Carl Josef Leiprecht, Bishop of Rottenburg. He was active in the Council's commission which discussed matters relating to life in the Orders. life. Friedrich Wulf SJ, a specialist in matters relating to the Orders and director of *Geist und Leben*; Paul Pfister SJ, professor of theology in Tokyo; Cardinal E.Ruffini, Archbishop of Palermo.

44. Paul Rusch, Bishop of Innsbruck. The protest was against the fact that Patriarch Maximus IV Saigh wanted to speak French and not Latin in the Council in order to put on record that the church was not Latin. Archbishop P.Felici was General Secretary of the Council and not above the moderators, like Döpfner. K.Mörsdorf, professor of canon law in Munich. J. Höffner was then Bishop of Münster. J.Salaverri SJ, Spanish conciliar theologian; M.Maccarone, Italian conciliar theologian; G.Martelet SJ, French conciliar theologian.

45. T.Maunz, at that time Bavarian minister of culture.

46. Rahner's sixtieth birthday.

47. Heinz Schuster, responsible with the Dutch publisher Paul Brand for the foundation of *Concilium*, editor of the *Handbuch der Pastoraltheologie*, now Professor of Theology in Saarbrücken. E.Florit was Cardinal Archbishop of Florence.

For Further Reading

A full listing of Karl Rahner's works is to be found as following:

'Die Bibliographie Karl Rahner 1924–1964', which originally appeared in the Festschrift *Gott in Welt*, has now been produced in a separate volume, edited by R.Bleistein and E. Klinger, and extended to cover the period up to 1969; it is published by Herder Verlag. This bibliography has been further extended in 'Bibliographie Karl Rahner 1969–1974', a pamphlet edited by R.Bleistein and published by Herder Verlag. This listing also contains titles of works which are discussions of Rahner's theology; the volume *Christentum innerhalb und ausserhalb der Kirche*, ed. E.Klinger, contains a great many more titles of works about Karl Rahner.

Publications by and about Karl Rahner for the period between 1974 and 1979 are listed in the Festschrift *Wagnis Theologie* and those between 1979 and the beginning of 1984 in the Festschrift *Glaube im Prozess*.

The Rahner bibliography was arranged from the start in such a way that Rahner's original publications, translations of his books, new impressions and reprints, and titles in which he was involved as editor, were listed in sequence and given a through numbering. For better or worse, this principle has been retained throughout the supplements. Titles overlooked have been inserted at the right chronological point with a, b, c, etc. Thus at the beginning of 1984 the listing amounted to 3998 titles, not counting those marked a, b, c, and 948 titles of books discussing Rahner.

The impression given by this listing is chaotic, and Karl Rahner bears some responsibility, because of the way in which he allowed this evaluation of his articles. As the same work can occur several times in the listing – sometimes just with another title – and this in fact happens often, a revised list would contain very many fewer than 4000 titles. However, that does not detract from the enormous number of Rahner's publications.

'An English Bibliographical Aid to Karl Rahner' by C.J.Pedley appeared in the *Heythrop Journal* 25, 1984, 319–65, with an additional note and comment in the *Heythrop Journal* 26, 1985, 310–18. I am grateful to the Librarian of Heythrop College, Michael Walsh, for this information.

In the first part of my own short book I have attempted to indicate the best way of approaching Karl Rahner. The interviews which he gave in the last years of his life are useful for understanding him (see p.185, n.2). In them he spoke spontaneously and openly about the driving force behind his spirituality and theology and also made comments on his life. The extended interview with Meinold Krauss, *I Remember*, Crossroad Publishing Company, New York and SCM Press, London 1985, published separately, is particularly valuable here.

Extracts from Rahner's writings are collected in two useful works: *The Practice of Faith*, Crossroad Publishing Company 1983 and SCM Press 1985, which is particularly concerned with his spirituality, and *A Rahner Reader*, edited by Gerald McCool, Seabury Press and Darton, Longman and Todd 1975, is more orientated on his theology.

Of course the essential material for further study is contained in *Theological Explorations*. In part the numbering of the volumes of the English translation differs from that of the German original *Schriften zur Theologie*: for convenience a paralled listing is given here.

Theological Explorations	*Schriften zur Theologie*
1	1
2	2
3	3
4	4
5	5
6	6
7	7.1
8	7.2
9	8.1
10	8.2
11	9.1
12	9.2
13	10.1
14	10.2
15	11
16	12.1
17	12.2
18	13.1
19	13.2 and some of 14
20	14 selected articles from 14

Where titles in the text are given in English and printed in italics, an English translation of the work exists.

Index